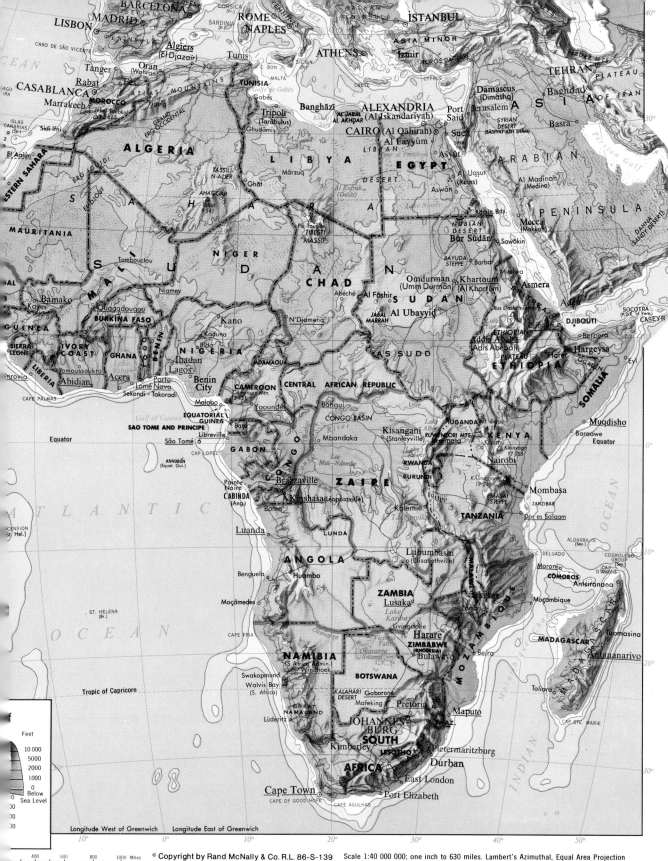

Enchantment of the World

GHANA

By Martin Hintz

Consultant for Ghana: Immanuel Wallerstein, Ph.D., Distinguished Professor, Department of Sociology, State University of New York, Binghamton, New York

Consultant for Reading: Robert L. Hillerich, Ph.D., Bowling Green State University, Bowling Green, Ohio

40101

ⲤⲢ CHILDRENS PRESS ®

CHICAGO

In the busy market at Kumasi, vegetables (above) and ornate loaves of bread (opposite page) are just a few of the products to be found.

To Peter, who *is* learning about himself

Library of Congress Cataloging-in-Publication Data

Hintz, Martin.
  Ghana.

  (Enchantment of the world)
  Includes index.
  Summary: Presents an overview of Ghana, including
its geography, history, industry, economy, and
customs.
  1. Ghana—Juvenile literature.   [1.   Ghana]
I. Title. II. Series.
DT510.H56   1987   966.7   86-29935
ISBN 0-516-02773-5

Childrens Press, Chicago

Picture Acknowledgments
© **Robert Frerck, Odyssey Productions:** Pages 4, 5, 6 (top),
24, 37 (right), 42 (top), 58 (bottom), 62 (top), 69 (2 photos),
74 (left), 84 (left), 85 (right), 90 (top left and bottom right),
100 (2 photos), 101 (right), 102, 107 (top left and center)
© **Beryl Goldberg:** Pages 6 (bottom), 9, 11 (2 photos), 13,
25 (right), 82, 84 (right), 92 (2 photos), 93 (left)

© **Dave G. Houser:** Pages 12, 27 (right), 30, 58 (top left), 62
(bottom, left and right), 64 (left), 85 (left), 86 (right), 90
(bottom left), 93 (right), 101 (left), 104 (top left)
Tom Stack & Associates: © Janet M. Milhomme: Pages 14,
17, 23, 56 (bottom), 90 (top right), 94 (2 photos), 95 (right),
96 (2 photos)
Photo Researchers, Inc.: © John Moss: Page 18, 119; © Tom
McHugh: Page 28 (bottom right); © Victor Englebert: Page
33; © Stephanie Dinkins: Page 34; © Thomas D.W.
Friedmann: Page 99 (left); © Pamela Johnson Meyer: Page
103
© **Hutchinson Library:** Cover, Pages 42 (bottom), 59
(right), 64 (right), 70, 73, 86 (left), 95 (left), 107 (right);
© Ann Tully: Pages 19, 54, 60, 77 (right), 89, 99 (right), 104
(bottom)
Bruce Coleman Incorporated: Page 27 (left); © Norman
Myers: Pages 20, 104 (top right), 111; © Dale & Marian
Zimmerman: Page 28 (top), © Kim Taylor, Page 28 (bottom
left); © John Elk III: Pages 37 (left), 40, 56 (top), 58 (top
right), 59 (left), 67 (left), 75
Root Reosurces: © Loren M. Root: Page 25 (left); © Mary
Albright: Page 29; © Jane P. Downton: Page 74 (right)
Historical Pictures Service, Chicago: Pages 38, 46
Associated Press/World Wide: Pages 49, 51 (2 photos), 52,
53, 55, 106
© **Photri:** Pages 61, 81
© **American Museum of Natural History:** Page 77 (left);
© O. Bauer/J. Beckett: Page 79
Len W. Meents: Maps on pages 57, 62, 67
**Courtesy Flag Research Center, Winchester,
Massachusetts 01890:** Flag on back cover
Courtesy Embassy of Ghana, 68 (right)
Cover: Drums and dancing—part of a festival

TABLE OF CONTENTS

Traveling by bus is one of the principle means of commuting.
The buses may be crowded, but it is still possible to carry freight on the top.

Chapter 1

A DAY WITH MICHAEL

Michael Kofi Mensah glanced at the sky. It was sullen with fat thunderclouds that made the early morning gloomy. Rain threatened to fall any minute. Michael and his friend Thomas, who were standing together at the bus stop, weren't worried. They were glad that the storm was threatening. Their fathers' farms desperately needed the rain. Although it was not harvesting time, the maize (corn) was drying to rustling stalks.

Other people at the bus stop also looked at the low clouds and discussed the weather. That seemed to be the most important topic of conversation. It was the time of the midyear drought in Ghana, a regular occurrence. But this year the drought had lasted longer and was more severe. Already the crops had been affected. The harvest would not be as large as the farmers had hoped.

Michael and Thomas agreed that rain, any rain, would be good. But it wasn't just the lack of rain that worried them. Dangerous brushfires were spreading. The heavy smoke north of their village was as thick as the clouds. It had obscured the sun for days, probably from blazes set by hunters on the grasslands.

Finally, the boys' red and white bus grunted to a stop at the corner. Dust and engine exhaust made Michael cough and cover his eyes. But he ducked his head and jumped aboard, paying his fare. Michael and Thomas lived in a small village, so they had to ride the bus ten miles (sixteen kilometers) to their district school. The lumbering vehicle made regular trips along the main highway near Michael's home, picking up other schoolchildren. Adults also rode the bus, on the way to market or work.

The chatter in the bus was loud, especially from the children. If they weren't talking about the weather, they were discussing the upcoming soccer match in the huge stadium in Accra, Ghana's capital. The Ghanaian national team was going to play a team from the Ivory Coast, Ghana's neighbor to the west. Of course, Michael and Thomas hoped their team would win. They would not be able to attend the match, but they intended to listen to it on the radio.

Finally the bus arrived at the school. The crowd of pupils tumbled off. The grown-ups breathed a sign of relief. The quiet was welcome.

Michael and Thomas raced to the school door. It was almost 8:30 A.M., and class would start in a few minutes. The hallways in the school were covered with drawings and paintings. A large trophy case was near the director's office. It was full of prizes and awards won by school teams in sports, music, and debates.

Michael and Thomas squeezed into their desks just as Mrs. Bekoe, their teacher, rang the opening bell. The first class of the day was English. Because there are four major languages in Ghana and many dialects spoken, learning English is important. It is the official language of the country.

The class exchanges letters and drawings with children their own age at a school in London. Writing is good practice for learning how to use English correctly.

Schoolchildren from the northern city of Bolgatanga

Like most pupils in their school, Michael and Thomas belong to the Ga ethnic group. Their people live primarily on the coastal plains in southern Ghana. However, one of their classmates is an Ada and two others are Shai. Mrs. Bekoe is an Asante, whose family still lives in central Ghana.

The southern section of Ghana was controlled by Europeans for more than a century, and history is important to each citizen. Mrs. Bekoe says that by knowing their past, the young people of Ghana will be able to deal with the present and look forward to the future.

The boys are proud of their ethnic and linguistic heritage. Yet their teacher stresses that all the ethnic groups in Ghana are equally important. Each has contributed to the colorful mosaic that makes up the country today.

There are many different ethnic groups living in Ghana today. Ghanaians do not have tensions between the ethnic groups, in fact a conscious effort has been made to unite all the people. Whenever the class takes a trip, whether it is to the national capital to visit a museum or to the busy port of Tema, Mrs. Bekoe reminds them that they should be proud of their country and its accomplishments.

Mathematics and geography followed English class. Then it was time for recess. By now, the storm clouds had drifted off without even a sprinkle to dampen the dust. That was disappointing, but it meant the boys and their pals could play soccer outside and dangle from the huge tire swings. Michael also liked to play a game he called "grab it." Teams of three or more players stand in a row facing each other across the playground. A ball is placed between them. At a signal, two members from each team run toward the ball. They have to pick up the ball without being touched by the other team. If a player is snared, the opponent who does the touching scores a point for his team. If a player can pick up the ball without being touched, his team scores a point.

By the time recess was over, everyone was puffing hard. But there were still more classes before lunch. A study hour followed lunch, then came art and music sessions. Since farming was so important in their district, agricultural classes were taught in the middle school. During the last school session, the pupils worked in the school garden. It was not too hot by then and they could go home to wash rather then return to their classroom. The garden had maize, yams, chili peppers, and a variety of other vegetables. Finally the day was over and everyone headed for home.

At home Michael had after-school chores. He cleaned the chicken pen, milked the goats, and carried water from the village's

Above: A Ghanaian boy does chores at home after school.
Below: Schoolgirls work on their garden project.

Local residents use the public well near Bolgatanga.

central well to his house. His younger sister and brother had been playing all day. They were too young to go to school. Michael remembered those lucky days when he could fish or romp with his dog.

He quickly finished his tasks and tackled his homework without being reminded, because it was a special night. That evening, the district fire warden and a representative from the Ghanaian department of forestry were going to be in Michael's village. They were going to show films about the proper use of fire in clearing brush for cultivation, a traditional way of opening up new land to plant crops. Also, many of the farmers had questions about how to deal with the drought. They hoped the government officials would have some helpful advice.

The mobile film truck was already in the village compound. A screen was set up near the Catholic mission church where Michael

A section of a field that has been burned to clear it for planting.

and his family attended Sunday mass. The show would start as soon as it was dark. All the children were very excited. So were their parents.

Because this was a special occasion, Michael's mother had prepared *adua froi* (bean stew) for supper. It was Michael's favorite meal. He liked to watch her preparing it. First she soaked black-eyed beans for an hour and then cooked the beans until they were soft. Next, she fried onions in a pan coated with palm oil. For a special touch, tomatoes were added to the bubbling oil. Then the soft beans were added. Finally she added some dried fish to the concoction, and let it simmer for a while. *Adua froi* is eaten with rice, yams, or fried plantain, which is similar to a banana. But no one lingered over their supper. They wanted to see the movies.

The films and the lectures were helpful and everyone learned a great deal from the government workers. After the films, sweets were passed around the crowd. By the end of the show, Michael was almost asleep. But he helped carry his little sister home to bed. His father lifted Michael's brother and lugged him off.

Tomorrow would be another day.

A section of the Mampong Scarp can be seen in the distance.

Chapter 2

A DIVERSE NATION

The Republic of Ghana is almost a perfect rectangle. It lies in the southern portion of West Africa, which is larger than the continental United States. Modern Ghana covers 92,100 square miles (238,537 square kilometers), about the size of Great Britain or the state of Missouri. Its widest distance from east to west measures about 310 miles (499 kilometers) and from north to south it is 445 miles (716 kilometers) long.

To the east is the nation of Togo, beyond which are Benin and the Republic of Nigeria. To the west is the Ivory Coast. To the north is Burkina Faso. Ghana's irregular southern coastline stretches 335 miles (539 kilometers).

TOPOGRAPHY

Ghana has gently rolling hills. More than 50 percent of Ghana is less than 500 feet (152 meters) above sea level. The Togo Range extends from the south near Accra, eastward into Togo. Another range, the Kwahu Scarp, cuts off the lower third of Ghana from the north, running from the cities of Koforidua to Wenchi. Beyond this ridge of rolling landscape is the Afram Plains.

There also are some low hills in far northwestern Ghana. These hills have steep slopes and are called scarps. The Mampong Scarp, the Kwahu Scarp, and the Ejura Scarp look like walls of a fort when they are seen from a distance.

In the northern regions of West Africa are the creeping, whispering sands of the Sahara Desert, edging farther south each year. The desert is growing because of drought and overuse of land for crops and grazing. On the south is the rolling surf and treacherous undertows of the Gulf of Guinea. Both are equally dangerous.

THE SURF

The roaring surf always made landings by ship very risky. Huge sandbars would build up where the rivers meet the ocean, preventing large sailing ships from approaching close to shore. However, the inland merchants shipped their goods to the sea by means of the rivers. Canoes or surfboats then had to be used to ferry the trade items to the European vessels offshore.

In 1602, Dutch trader Pieter de Marees wrote how small boats used the morning wind to blow them out from the land. By noon, however, the wind shifted and headed toward shore. The canoeists had to have their boats loaded and ready to return by then or risk being swamped.

Frenchman John Barbot wrote in his journal in 1732 that only the "most fit and experienced men" could manage to paddle canoes over the bars and backwaters along the coast. It took a great deal of dexterity to carry the canoes through without being overturned, sunk, or split to pieces.

In 1887, engineer Archer P. Groch took a surfboat ride on his first visit to the Gold Coast, as the area was known then. The paddlers waited at the crest of a breaker, tense and ready to row at

Fishermen heading out into the surf

The boatswain holds the steering rudder while the others paddle.

the signal of the crew chief, called a boatswain. He would be balanced in the rear of the boat, holding the steering rudder. At the proper time, just after the wave began breaking, he would urge the canoe forward. Everyone paddled as hard as possible to get across the sandbar before the next wave could catch them. After getting across the bar, the boat still had about sixty feet (eighteen meters) to shore. The rolling surf carried it up to the beach. Groch said the boat hit the land so hard that almost everyone was knocked out of their seat.

Obviously, this dangerous process was never really satisfactory for handling large amounts of trade. In order to accommodate modern vessels, ports had to be constructed and maintained.

THE NORTH

In the northern savanna of Ghana, there are only two seasons, wet and dry. During the rainy season, only 30 to 45 inches (71 to

Washing and bathing in the Volta River

114 centimeters) of rain falls. This season is followed by the dry season, which lasts from November to March. Here the vegetation is primarily tall grass and low trees. The days are hot, but the nights are cool.

RIVERS AND LAKES

In some bad years, such as 1973 and 1983, when there is less than normal rain in the north and central parts of Ghana, the country is lucky to have enough of water in its lower half. The country is well drained by the Volta River system, which flows south through Ghana. The Black, Red, and White arms of the massive river move down from the north and join about 300 miles (483 kilometers) from the sea. The rushing waters of the Volta pour into the sea about 50 miles (80 kilometers) east of Accra.

Other major rivers, such as the Tano, Ankobra, and Pra, flow

The hydroelectric dam at Akosombo

from the central hills directly south to the sea. None of these rivers is consistently high. During the dry season, they are mud flats.

Ghana can boast of one of the largest man-made lakes in the world. The giant hydroelectric dam at Akosombo has backed up the Volta waters for more than 200 miles (322 kilometers) to form Lake Volta. Lake Volta is deep enough for large motorboats carrying goods and passengers along its entire length. It also is used for commercial fishing.

The largest natural lake is Lake Bosumtwi, near the city of Kumasi in central Ghana. It lies in an enormous crater believed to have been the bed of an ancient volcano. The entire district is a great tourist attraction because of its beautiful scenery.

CLIMATE

Ghana is a tropical nation. It can get very hot and sticky with the high humidity that blankets the country. The city of Tamale in the north has registered temperatures as high as 107 degrees Fahrenheit (42 degrees Celsius). Generally, the temperatures hover around the mid-eighties.

Southern Ghana has two wet and two dry seasons. Because the temperature is so constant, it is hard to predict when one or the other season is about to begin. Sometimes, however, there are surprises. The month that is supposed to be wettest turns out to be dry. Generally the most rain falls between March and July. It is dry throughout August and from December to February.

Ghana has to contend with the blustery *harmattan*, a hot, dry, northeasterly wind that howls across the Sahara. Although it lowers the humidity, it bakes everything in its path. From December to February, the windblown sand from the desert seeps in everywhere. The windy nights are generally cool, which gives relief for sleeping.

The Ghanaian rain pattern is strange in another way. On the far western coast, near Axim, more than 80 inches (203 centimeters) might soak the landscape in a year. Toward Accra, the farmers are lucky to get 30 inches (76 centimeters) a year. Rainfall is highest in the southwest corner of Ghana, averaging from 50 to 86 inches (127 to 218 centimeters). The southeast has the same rainy seasons, but generally less annual rain, about 30 inches (76 centimeters). In the north, rainfall averages between 44 and 50 inches (112 to 127 centimeters) and occurs in a single April to September season. This is followed by a long dry season.

The mean annual temperature in Ghana is 80 degrees Fahrenheit (29 degrees Celsius).

VEGETATION

Naturally the weather affects the vegetation. Grass and scrubland are in the east and north, which receive less rain. Tropical forests thickly coat much of the central section and the west. The lowlands are swampy. At one time, almost all of Ghana probably was covered by what botanists call the high forest. This type of forest is made up of tall, straight trees with broad, leafy overhead cover.

While these green oceans of trees might appear strong and powerful, they are really fragile ecosystems. The rich plant life here depends on shallow, fertile topsoil, rather than deep soil. When the trees are removed, the topsoil can be endangered. This is true if farmers don't allow the land to recover its fertility after using it for several years. The exhausted soil should be allowed to rest, or lay fallow. During the resting period, the leaves fall from the covering vegetation. They rot and form a natural fertilizer. This helps the soil recover its strength. If the soil can't do that, it is soon depleted. Continual use of the land means that chemical fertilizers must be used.

Tropical forests, such as those found in Ghana, are among the oldest types of vegetation remaining in the world. Trees similar to those growing thousands of years ago have been discovered. Once the tropical forest is cut down, it takes generations to grow back— if it ever can. Therefore, Ghana has wisely established reserves to ensure that some forest will be protected for future generations. But is is hard not to exploit the natural resources found in the

A worker in the lumber industry

forests. Lumbering is an important industry. Wood is needed to build homes, schools, and hospitals and to make paper and furniture. It is used also for fuel.

The timber cutters often damaged surrounding vegetation when they removed valuable trees, such as ebony and mahogany. When chopped down, the huge trees toppled over and crushed the smaller varieties. The valuable trees are scattered throughout the forest and are hard to reach. So roads had to be chopped through the undergrowth, causing more destruction. In addition, before the forest reserves were established, land needed for expanded fields and cocoa plantations was carved out of the woodland.

Currently, the forest reserve cannot be used to grow crops unless people who live nearby are starving. Special permits are

Sausage (left) and baobob (right) trees

needed to clear trees for farmland. After a certain time, the farmer must replant trees to replace those he cut down.

Forest devastation is very evident around the gold and manganese mines, where the trees have been cut for poles, firewood, and timber. Air pollution and refuse from the mines also has killed much of the brush. Good sized trees can rarely be found around the entrance to the mine pits.

However there are many varieties of trees in Ghana. The exotic dawadawa, anogeissu, and shea grow in the savanna. Ancient, fat baobobs, as well as tamarind, with their yellow flowers and brown seed pods, are common around the northern villages and cities. Many of these trees have thick hides of bark, which are a protection against fire.

FIRES AND THE ENVIRONMENT

For centuries, setting fires has been a traditional way of clearing land in Ghana. Hunters also make a ring of fire around their quarry. The fire drives the animals together, making them easier to kill. These brushfires can encourage new green growth, but their excessive use eventually damages the new and old plants. Without a vegetation cover, there is erosion of the topsoil from wind and rain.

Often fires that are carelessly set burn out of control for days. They sweep across the savanna destroying everything. Some fires are set by youngsters attempting to smoke big rats and other rodents called "grass cutters" out of their holes. If the children aren't careful, the blaze can spread and endanger entire villages.

The Ghanaian government is becoming more conscious of the need to protect the landscape. Fire wardens have been appointed in the villages by the department of forestry. Their job is to educate others to the danger of fire, as well as to report the careless use of fires. The wardens have already made a helpful impact in Ghana.

Forest rangers receive training at school such as the one located at Sunyani, the capital of the Brong-Ahafo district. The rangers must study for four years before being certified. They are taught biology, soil science, agricultural economics, forest management, and social studies.

In tune with today's concern about the environment, the University of Science and Technology in Kumasi was established in 1983. The Ghanaian government expects the graduates of the institute to be the leaders in protecting the country's natural gifts.

Lemurs (left) are found in the high forest and giraffes (right) live in the Mole Game Preserve.

ANIMALS, WILDLIFE, AND INSECTS

Seven national parks, three game reserves, and two wildlife sanctuaries protect indigenous African wildlife. Actually, there are few large wild animals remaining in Ghana.

Elephants were once plentiful, but now have almost disappeared. Growing use of their natural feeding grounds for agriculture has pushed them away. Lions and leopards are rarely encountered, although an occasional hyena or jackal may kill some livestock. Buffalo, antelope, and wild hogs are protected in the game preserves. Several species of monkeys swing overhead in the remaining high forest, including the chimpanzee and lemur.

Dangerous snakes, such as the cobra and black mamba, are found throughout Ghana. In addition to the fire hazard, parents don't like children to smoke out rat holes because of the danger of snakes. Sometimes, a huge angry snake, up to seven feet (two meters) long, can slither out of such a hole and attack the children. Every year, people die from snakebite.

Lovely butterflies (top) are found in Ghana, as well as the menacing tsetse fly (above left) and the cobra (right).

Hippos like the mud and pools in the wet flatlands.

In addition to the crocodiles in the rivers, hippopotamuses wallow in the wet flatlands. They love the mud and pools.

Many species of brilliantly colored butterflies flit along the forest belt near the coast.

The tsetse fly is an unwelcome pest to Ghana. Its bite causes the dreaded sleeping sickness, which has devastated much of Africa over the centuries. The disease, which affects the brain and causes fever, puts the victim into a coma. It may be fatal. However, this illness is not as prevalent as it is in East Africa.

Shorthorn cattle also are bothered by the tsetse flies. They have built up a partial immunity to the disease called trypanosomiasis, but they are chronically affected.

Ghanaians also have to put up with unfriendly mosquitoes, which carry malaria, and chigger fleas.

Ghanaians are concerned about their land. They realize that it is part of their past, present, and future.

Rivers and coastal lagoons have always been used for transportation. Ancient stone tools have been found here.

Chapter 3

FROM KINGDOM

TO COLONY

Ghana has always been at the center of human activity in West Africa. Archaeologists have found ancient stone choppers and other tools buried deep under Ghana's modern landscape. They date back thousands and thousands of years. Many of these implements have been discovered along the banks of the White Volta River, in north-central Ghana. Scientists believe that early people there preferred to live in the grasslands, where it was easier to hunt prey than in the dense jungles.

Stone tools dating from later periods have been found elsewhere in the country, usually along waterways.

STONE AGE CULTURES

These earliest Stone Age cultures are divided into several waves: Chellean, Acheulian, Sangoan, and Kalinian. The migrations of people from the north and east began at least forty thousand years ago. Next came other ethnic groups: the Lupembans and Aterians. One mysterious group might have come from North Africa. Their axes, arrowheads, and blades are similar to those found in the Nile Valley of Egypt.

All these people wandered back and forth across the West African landscape, leaving evidence of their passing scattered from riverbank to forest edge. Caves and rock overhangs made good homes. If the people were hungry, they simply had to forage for roots and wild berries. Sometimes they planted crops, but moved to new territories after only a season or two. They were probably peaceful hunters. They raised cattle, the ancestors of today's Hamitic longhorn or Ndama cattle. Trade was a major feature of their lives and they lived by bartering. In fact, some stone tool "factories" have been discovered. At these sites, goods that could be exchanged for items made by neighbors were produced.

MIGRATORY PEOPLE AND EARLY SETTLEMENTS

Sometime after 500 B.C. iron working became known in West Africa. Immigrants from the Sahara Desert came into the area. Their iron weapons easily pushed aside the Stone Age culture. These people settled wherever there was water. They didn't mind the high forest. Their fire-tempered knives and spears were more than a match for the large animals in the jungle.

Ghana was not an easy land to cross. The forests were sometimes an impenetrable barrier. The people would clear some land for their farms, but they would move on when the soil was worn out. Often they would simply displace another ethnic group and take over everything that the first people had built and cultivated.

This was the pattern of life throughout West Africa for subsequent centuries. Ghana did not have any set geographical borders. Of course, there were vague territorial frontiers that often

Early inhabitants of Ghana could settle and farm and
when the soil was worn out, they would move on.

overlapped and were disputed by various local chiefs. Generally,
however, people simply followed their herds or tracked the wild
game. There were only a few fortified villages.

Eventually, by the 1200s, some ethnic groups settled in southern
Ghana. They liked the mixture of grasslands and forests along the
coast. Populations multiplied. The people who spoke the same
language generally stayed in the same region. Those that spoke
Akan controlled most of the western third of what is now modern
Ghana. The Ga-Adangbe were in the south, the Ewe in the east,
and the Mole-Daghane speakers in the northeast.

THE ANCIENT KINGDOM OF GHANA

The ancient kingdom of Ghana was about 500 miles (805
kilometers) northwest of the present-day nation of Ghana. It
flourished along the Niger River before the Sahara Desert reached
its long, dry fingers that far south. Ghana was a highly
sophisticated economic and military center from the fourth

*Painting designs on cotton with a small stick
and liquid from the bark of a tree is an old tradition
that is still practiced in Ghana.*

to the tenth centuries. Arab historians wrote that its first forty-four kings were white. That interpretation is now understood to mean that the rulers were most likely brown-skinned Berbers, any one of a number of northern African people.

Researchers now suggest that a bloody revolution occurred in the eighth century, in which the Berbers were overthrown and replaced by black African monarchs. The new kings were of the Soninke branch of the Mandingo race, who ruled until 1076. In that year, the kingdom of Ghana was attacked and fell under the onslaught of other North Africans. Refugees fleeing the new invaders migrated down to what is present-day Ghana.

The ensuing dynasty became a great trading nation over the next century, using gold, ivory, animal skins, cotton, and kola nuts. There was a noted university in Timbuktu where scholars gathered to study medicine, philosophy, and mathematics.

THE EMPIRE OF MALI

But even this empire began to decay. Fierce nomads from farther north kept chipping away at its borders. Many of its inhabitants fled farther south. The Empire of Mali eventually conquered ancient Ghana, growing to be the largest and most noteworthy of all the kingdoms of West Africa, from the thirteenth to the seventeenth century. The kings of Mali were Muslims, followers of the Arabic prophet Muhammad.

Mansa Musa was the most powerful of the Mali kings. He ruled for twenty-five years. Legends relate how he once traveled throughout his kingdom to see the extent of his territory. Accompanied by sixty thousand courtiers and guards, plus twelve thousand slaves, he spent months marching from city to city. He supposedly gave more than 3,000 pounds (1,360 kilograms) of gold as gifts to subchiefs or as alms to beggars.

Like the Ghanaian kingdom that preceded it, the Mali empire eventually grew weak. It became easy prey for neighboring kingdoms, such as Songhai.

THE SONGHAI KINGDOM

The Songhai kingdom originated as a small territory south of the Niger River, eventually moving its capital to Gao. In the fifteenth century the Songhai became the dominant kingdom in West Africa. But at the bloody battle of Tondibi in 1591, the Songhai empire was crushed under the onslaught of Moors led by the Moroccan prince El Mansur.

CLANS AND ETHNIC GROUPS

Fiercely anti-Muslim, the refugees who fled from Ghana and Mali were slowly consolidated into clans, which eventually became ethnic and linguistic groups. Many units united under one leader to form a nation. This was probably the process that brought together the powerful Asantes, one of the Akan people. The first Akan state, Bono, was established before 1300, probably drawing on governmental experiences learned in ancient Ghana. The government had tax collectors, treasurers, and executioners.

These early Ghanaians formed the beginnings of the ninety-two different ethnic groups in modern Ghana. Thirty-four separate languages are still spoken. This language diversity creates communication problems for business and the government.

Over the years, many of these ethnic clusters grew strong and expanded their power. For instance, the Gonja kingdom was made up of several clans north of the Black Volta River. They captured the saltworks in the area, settled down, and became great traders.

The Asante people eventually clustered around Lake Bosumtwi. They built Asantemanso, a large town that tradition says had exactly seventy-seven streets. Because they were so close to the great lake tucked in the bottom of a volcanic crater, their folktales say that the first Asante popped out of that huge hole in the ground. He liked the neighborhood so much, he stayed above the surface of the earth.

THE GOLD COAST

Other visitors to Ghana didn't come from the underworld. They came from the sea. The Portuguese arrived in 1471, landing on the

A section of Castle of Sao Jorge da Mina at Elmina (left) and a bronze Portuguese warrior (right) from the National Museum in Accra

level coast between the Ankobra and Volta rivers. So much gold was obtained from this region that the Portuguese named it "El Mina" meaning "mine." The principal city there is still called Elmina. French explorers called the district "Côte d'Or," or the Gold Coast. That was its name throughout the colonial era until independence in 1957 when it became Ghana.

The Portuguese wanted to monopolize this rich gold trade, so they built the massive Castle of Sao Jorge da Mina at Elmina. Other forts were constructed at Axim, Shama, and Accra. At first, the Europeans were content to trade for gold, ivory, and pepper.

A raid on a village on market day to capture slaves

THE SLAVE TRADE

However, the colonization of the Americas and the establishment of cotton and sugar plantations in the New World had an evil effect on this commerce. The demand for cheap labor exploded. It was decided that manpower needs in the new colonies could easily be filled by slaves.

Black Africans were considered better able to adapt to the heat and humidity found in the Caribbean and on North and South American plantations. Therefore, many people were brutally plucked from the interior of Africa and hauled in chains to the coast. From there, they were placed on slave ships and taken away. Many died before they reached their intended destination.

There had always been slaves in West Africa. However, they

were generally used as domestic help and were usually well cared for. It was certainly not a gentle or humane system, but it was nothing like the horrible trade that developed when the Europeans arrived.

EUROPEAN ENCROACHMENT

Other whites envied the Portuguese hold on the African coast. Dutch, English, French, Danes, Swedes, and Germans subsequently came to Ghana. They bickered, battled, and bled over who would control the gold and slave trade.

As the European influence grew, the local Ghanaians adopted new ways of doing things. Some were good. They learned to cultivate crops; such as sugarcane, maize, bananas, tobacco, lemons, oranges, red pepper, and pineapples. Pigs and sheep were brought into Ghana.

Yet, like slavery for export, other unsavory elements were introduced into Ghanaian life. Diseases brought by the Europeans devastated the coast, wiping out entire villages. If a Ghanaian lived to be fifty years old, he or she was considered a lucky person. Infant mortality was very high, as it was in all parts then.

Of course, native African illnesses killed off many Europeans. It was almost like a revenge. If a settler could live in Ghana for at least two months without dying of malaria, which he got from the bite of the mosquito, he was considered fortunate. Once that hurdle was past, the white person had a good chance of staying alive in the tropics.

To get the gold and slaves, the Europeans would trade linens, silk, beads, copper and brass, guns and gunpowder, and alcohol.

Fort William on Cape Coast was built in 1835.

From far offshore, just beyond the pounding surf, they would unload goods from their sailing ships into canoes. The powerful waves prevented the vessels from getting close to land. But the dangers were ignored because such huge profits could be made. Port cities such as Elmina, Cape Coast, and Christianborg became important because they were commercial power centers. That's where the money was.

Many royal Ghanaians grew rich by working alongside the Europeans or by demanding bribes. They would hire out their people as porters and armed guards to accompany the caravans into the interior. The Denkyira, Fanti, Akwamu, and Asante people were recognized as shrewd businessmen who could drive a hard bargain. Trade routes snaked through the countryside, with each section of the trail controlled by one or the other of the ethnic groupings.

ABOLISHMENT OF THE SLAVE TRADE

By the early 1800s, the slave trade with Europe and America began to wane. Britain's Parliament outlawed slavery in 1807, but it was only an initial step in halting this horrible traffic. Other nations weren't as concerned. They continued to buy slaves whenever they could, running the blockading gauntlet of British warships. Often, when hotly pursued, the slaver would toss his human cargo overboard in order to destroy the "evidence." It wasn't until several generations after the British abolished slavery that the last slave ships sneaked out of West Africa and scurried across the Atlantic.

At first, many coastal chiefs objected to the abolishing of the slave trade, since their fortunes depended on it. When it was obvious that the British would not be deterred, the chiefs gradually began selling other trade items. At this time, there was a growing need in industrial Europe for raw materials from which to make soaps and lubricating oil. Palm oil was an excellent substitute for animal fat, and merchants soon found it more profitable to peddle oil than African slaves. By 1832, one former slaver was exporting more than 4,000 tons of oil annually.

Although the slave trade dwindled, most Westerners dealing in West Africa didn't care about medical or educational services to the people who lived around their outposts. But eventually, missionary societies came to Ghana to work with the people. This resulted in an entirely new way of life for many Ghanaian people.

European explorers settled on the coastline on the Gulf of Guinea.

Chapter 4

FROM COLONY TO INDEPENDENCE

The early centuries of European exploration primarily affected the coastline of Ghana. Few settlers moved inland. They were afraid of disease, wild animals, and the people who lived there. For the most part, the Europeans had good relations with the coastal chiefs. After all, both white and local blacks could profit from the trade in slaves and minerals. Europeans built forty-one forts along the seacoast to protect their economic interests. That was a fort almost every eight miles (thirteen kilometers).

MISSIONARY SOCIETIES

Usually the Europeans left the local chiefs alone and did not interfere with the people's tribal ways. However, by the mid 1800s, many missionary societies had established themselves in Ghana. They wanted the Ghanaians to become Christian. As people converted to Christianity, they gave up many of their traditions. ''Being European'' was considered a good thing.

This was unfortunate because much of the beautiful life-style of black Africa, from crafts to folktales, were lost in the rush to be like the white outsiders. However, on the other hand, many Ghanaians received excellent educations in Ghana and in Europe. Ghanaians gradually moved into professional jobs as missionaries, teachers, lawyers, administrators, military officers, doctors, and journalists.

The missionaries built schools. The Basel Mission Society established the Akropong Teacher Training College and the Aburi Girls' High School, as well as ninety others. Among the more than forty schools started by the Wesleyan Missionary Society was the famous Mfantsipim Secondary School in Cape Coast. Over the years, these schools produced some of Ghana's top leaders. The opportunity for higher education began when Achimota School in Accra was founded in 1930. It started as a secondary school, but soon introduced courses preparing students for entrance into the University of London. There Ghanaians could obtain degrees in various fields.

The missionaries were instrumental in helping end the slave trade. They worked hard to care for the local people and lobbied back home to have slavery outlawed. Their efforts eventually were successful as country after country officially opposed slavery.

EUROPEAN MERCHANTS

It became more profitable for Europeans to deal in palm oil, cotton, gold, rubber, and cocoa after the slave trade was abolished.

It is interesting to note that most of these efforts in education, medical services, and trade were done privately. The European governments seldom became involved.

The Danes left Ghana in 1850 and the Dutch pulled out in 1872. At first neither the Germans, who were generally merchants from Brandenburg, nor British had an official manner of governing their enclaves in Ghana.

In fact, a Scottish trader named George Maclean directed a committee of merchants who ran the day-to-day administrative affairs of the English settlements in the Gold Coast. He was given the title of governor of the Gold Coast, but was ordered not to interfere with the native states. So he had a problem. He had authority, but was told not to exercise it. Maclean solved his difficulty easily. He ignored the politicians back in Britain. After all, it was a long way from the mother country to Africa. He was concerned about the well-being of the people who lived outside the forts, although they were supposedly beyond his legal authority.

Maclean drew up a peace treaty with the Asante in 1831, which brought peace for about forty years after the first Asante War. Maclean tried legal cases that affected local life and even presided over local courts. He stationed merchant policemen along all trade routes to ensure that peace prevailed. Of course, all this was good for business. But it also meant that Ghana's coast remained calm during his term from 1830 to 1844.

BRITISH COLONIZATION

The British government didn't appreciate his efforts. It considered his activities illegal. A court of inquiry was set up in 1843, and the British brought its own administrators to Ghana. As one last act, Maclean concluded a treaty with Fanti chiefs along the coast in 1844. This strengthened the economic and political

Sir Garnet Wolseley led the British army against the Asante.

bonds between the Europeans and the local Fanti people. This is the famous Bond of 1844, which marks the beginning of effective colonization of the Gold Coast. It gave the British the incentive to push inland and topple the powerful Asante. The Fanti chiefs thought this was a great idea. They wanted to halt the Asante's competition for trade. So Fanti soldiers joined the red-coated British troops.

In the late 1800s, European powers grew hungrier for colonies. Their industries needed raw materials, which could be secured from underdeveloped and undefended territories. There was a rush to seize land in Asia and Africa, with little regard for the people who lived there.

In 1872, the British made the Gold Coast a crown colony, ignoring the treaties signed by Maclean. The proud Asante and their coastal allies were angry. They did not wish to be under the rule of the British. The powerful Asante confederation wanted to be left alone. They launched a bloody war. The British army under Sir Garnet Wolseley entered Kumasi in 1874 and both sides suffered heavy casualties. The Asante confederation was finally broken up in 1896. The British declared the northern territories of Ghana a protectorate and annexed the kingdom of Asante to the British Gold Coast in 1901. The Asante king, Agyeman Prempeh I, was exiled.

STIRRINGS FOR INDEPENDENCE

Meetings in Europe with the British, French, and Germans decided the boundaries of Ghana. No thought was given to the wishes and feelings of the people who lived there. After Germany was defeated in World War I, its African territory of Togoland, which bordered the Gold Coast, was divided equally between the British and French. The British administered their half of Togoland from Accra from 1918 to 1956.

Naturally, many Ghanaians wished for independence. As they grew economically stronger, they became more nationalistic. Ghanaians wanted a country of their own. Ghanaian workers complained about low wages and poor housing. Middle-class Ghanaian businessmen were angry about the competition from European, Syrian, and Indian traders in Ghana.

As Ghanaians became better educated, they could see the unfairness in the colonial system. They wondered why they had to leave their country to get a higher education. By 1948 only one university had been constructed in Ghana. The British apparently were afraid that higher education in their colonies would enlighten the students, causing them to ask for more and more reforms. The colonists feared that eventually the people might want independence.

Politics were also controlled by the British. Unlike the end of the 1890s, when many senior officials were native Ghanaians, in the later colonial years few native people had any positions of authority. In fact, in 1910, only two Ghanaians were minor civil servants out of 278 positions. This exclusion of Africans in government extended even through the 1940s.

To push for reforms, the Aborigines' Rights Protection Society was formed in 1896. It existed until 1925, when it was disbanded by the British governor. He convinced the chiefs that they did not need the help of the educated middle-class Ghanaians.

The formation of the West African National Congress, made up of native lawyers from all the British territories in West Africa, was significant also. From 1917 to 1930 the organization attempted to convince the British government that local universities were needed, that voting rights were necessary, and other reforms were necessary. The British were not ready to listen. They ignored the lawyers' demands.

When World War II started in 1939, many Ghanaians were conscripted into the British army. When the veterans returned home, they wondered why they were still considered second-class citizens in their own land. They asked why they could not have an independent nation.

Then there was a ray of hope. The newly formed United Nations stressed that people had a right to determine their own government. It also said that large and small nations were equal. The Ghanaians were excited about this promise for their future, especially since British Togoland became a United Nations trust territory in 1946. Many Ghanaians thought about independence.

This optimistic attitude was important. What had been a slow move away from colonization began to steamroll. The independence movement was led by the cream of Ghanaian intelligentsia. They formed the United Gold Coast Convention

Dr. J.B. Danquah was one of the founders of the United Gold Coast Convention. After Nkrumah became president in 1960, Danquah opposed his policies and was imprisoned.

(UGCC) in the early 1940s, under the leadership of Dr. J.B. Danquah, a lawyer. In 1947, the group asked Dr. Kwame Nkrumah to be its general secretary.

DR. KWAME NKRUMAH

Nkrumah, the son of a goldsmith, had been educated in mission schools. In 1939, he completed his studies at Pennsylvania's Lincoln University and became a lecturer in political science there, as well as becoming president of the African Student Organization of the United States and Canada. After postgraduate studies at the University of Pennsylvania, he went to England in 1945, where he helped organize the Pan-African Congress. When the UGCC invitation arrived, he decided that it was time to return to help his country's drive for independence.

But soon Nkrumah broke away from UGCC. He didn't agree with some of its ideas. Nkrumah formed his own political party in

1949, which he called the Convention People's party (CPP). Nkrumah was very active. He led strikes and boycotts against the British. He was jailed in 1950.

In 1951, a constitution that called for a legislature named by the people was written. Nkrumah was released that same year after his party swept the recently approved elections.

Nkrumah became prime minister of what was still called the Gold Coast in 1952. Two years later, on April 29, the Constitution was formally adopted and a cabinet composed entirely of Africans was established.

INDEPENDENCE

In 1956, a referendum was held in British Togo, which unified the Gold Coast and Togo (the French half of Togoland became free in 1960 and is now the Republic of Togo). Under Nkrumah's leadership, independence was finally granted on March 6, 1957, and he became prime minister. The country, now called Ghana, was the first black colony of British Africa to be freed.

THE REPUBLIC OF GHANA

When Ghana became a republic in 1960, Nkrumah became president. Everyone was excited. It was the dawn of a bright day. But this happy feeling dissolved quickly. Nkrumah was fearful of his opponents who used violent opposition, even assassination attempts. He put many in jail under the Preventive Detention Act. This law said that anyone charged with subversion could be imprisoned for five years without a trial. The sentence then could be extended to more five-year periods, as many as the government wished.

The citizens of Ghana were bitterly opposed to the harsh rule of President Nkrumah (right). On March 3, 1966 Ghanaians in Accra celebrated the overthrow of Nkrumah.

REBELLIONS AND COUPS

By 1964, Nkrumah had outlawed all political parties other than his own. The people were very unhappy. When Nkrumah was traveling in China in 1966, the Ghanaian army and police rebelled. The president and his cabinet were dismissed, the Convention People's party dissolved, and the constitution suspended. The revolt was supported by the Ghanaian people, especially when they saw Nkrumah's political prisoners freed.

The new military government called itself the National Liberation Council and was headed by General A.A. Afrifa. He

Dr. Kofi A. Busia became prime minister in 1969, but a military coup in January 1972 ousted him.

turned power over to civilian rule in October 1969, although he kept the title as chief of state until 1970.

In a special election in 1969, former Chief Justice Edward Akufo-Addo was named president and Dr. Kofi A. Busia became prime minister.

Economically Ghana was in bad shape. Ghanaian money was almost worthless. There was unrest. This resulted in another military coup in January 1972. Colonel I.K. Acheampong and other officers formed the National Redemption Council to govern Ghana. This was supposed to solve the country's problems.

But it didn't. The colonel wanted all the power. Again political parties were outlawed and people were imprisoned. Throughout 1977 and 1978, there were bloody demonstrations throughout Ghana. In 1978, Acheampong was arrested by General Frederick Akuffo. Akuffo then became head of state.

In 1979, Dr. Hilla Limann, a popular career diplomat from northern Ghana, became president—but not for long.

Akuffo wanted to return to a democratic form of government. But he was unable to solve the country's economic problems. In addition, there was corruption in the military. Senior officers were stealing money and living very well.

On June 4, 1979, Akuffo's government was overthrown by some junior officers led by Flight Lieutenant Jerry John Rawlings and the Armed Forces Revolutionary Council. Eight senior officers, including Acheampong, Akuffo, and Afrifa were executed. Dozens of other top administrators were jailed on corruption charges.

A rewritten constitution was signed on September 24, 1979. It allowed an elected president, a Parliament, and independent courts. The next president was Dr. Hilla Limann. He was new to politics, but was a popular career diplomat from northern Ghana. His People's National party respected individual rights and tried to do a good job. However, the Ghanaian economy worsened and

Jerry Rawlings and his council deposed President Limann December 31, 1981.

political corruption continued. The poor people protested when they saw how well the government officials were living. There was more turmoil in the streets.

On December 31, 1981, Rawlings and his council deposed President Limann and took over the government. Rawlings organized the Provisional National Defense Council and dissolved Parliament and suspended the constitution.

People were to exercise political power through "defense committees," that would determine policies. However, a small group of council leaders made most of the important decisions. In 1982, Rawlings's government said it would decentralize power. Regional and local secretaries were to have executive powers, with People's Defense Committees controlling local councils. However, by 1984, most authority was still held by the central council headquarters in Accra.

The ceremonial opening of the first of the first 198-member Ghanaian Parliament, which replaced the old 114-member House

THE FUTURE

Ghana is typical of other African nations moving along the rough road from colonization to independence. These new countries have had to overcome many economic and political difficulties. Sometimes they are successful, sometimes not. The degree of success depends greatly on the quality of their leaders.

There have been rapid changes: from colonial rule to independence; from civilian to military governments; from a capitalistic system to socialism. Currently, many of the country's economic problems remain unsolved. Yet with wise governing, Ghana can retain its place as an important voice in African affairs. But without enlightened government, the Ghanaian people will be the ultimate losers.

Accra, the capital, is on the coast. Liberty Avenue (above) and the central market (below) show what a busy, active city it is.

Chapter 5

GHANA OVERVIEW

ACCRA, THE CAPITAL

Accra, the capital, is the political and commercial soul of Ghana. It has long been a seat of power, especially for the ancient Ga people. Its established position along the coast made it an important port center for early European traders. Today, the city is busy and bustling with modern office and apartment buildings, wide boulevards, and well-stocked shops.

The fact that it did not have deep-water docking facilities did not bother the first Europeans who settled along the Gold Coast. They wanted to live in Accra because it was relatively cool and dry, free of some of the terrible tropical diseases. It was defensible, unlike some of the other towns along the coast. When it was under the authority of the Asante king, the area was relatively peaceful, although there were some minor clashes between ethnic groups over territorial boundaries.

Accra became the administrative center of the Gold Coast Crown Colony in 1876. The capital originally had been in Cape Coast, one of the earliest European settlements. But Europeans liked the open country north of Accra, so they decided to move the government offices.

Ghana has a warm climate. Lightweight clothing (above left) is worn on the street.
Below: The waterfront of Accra
Above right: The Supreme Court Building

Left: Modern office buildings in downtown Accra, with the Independence Monument in foreground
Right: The black star atop the monument symbolizes African freedom.

Accra originally consisted of several settlements: James Town, Ussher Town, and Osu. By 1885, the three were joined and the population grew. Today, there are about 840,000 people living in the city.

Many modern office buildings surround Accra's Black Star Square. Independence Day ceremonies every March 6 are held on the huge parade ground. Diplomats and government officials watch the festivities from a large reviewing platform. The Armed Forces Central Band always plays the national anthem, followed by the recitation of the national pledge. Schoolchildren usually put on a display of gymnastics and cultural groups perform in front of the dignitaries.

The Eternal Flame of African Liberation always burns in its huge black container in the square. It was lighted by Kwame Nkrumah as a reminder to Ghanaians that freedom is very precious.

The university in Legon

The capital is still a transportation hub for Ghana. Railroads and highways are like spiderwebs moving out from the city. Because of its connections and location, Accra was the West African headquarters of the United States Air Transport Command during World War II. Today, a modern international airport serves visitors.

Accra also hosts numerous meetings of African leaders and organizations. The West African Health Examination Board often has conferences in the city. This organization oversees public health inspectors and nurses in Ghana, Sierra Leone, and other African nations. The Ambassador Hotel, West Africa's first luxury hotel, had been used as a site for many such meetings. Its lobby is always crowded with colorful costumes and a blend of languages.

Docks at the port of Tema

THE PORT OF TEMA

While Accra itself remains the political and administrative
center of Ghana, the nearby port of Tema has taken the lead as the
commercial powerhouse. A new harbor was built in Tema in
1960. Many cocoa warehouses and processing plants are located
there. Trucks bring the cocoa to the government facilities where it
is graded and bagged. The cocoa is then loaded on ships for
transport to markets around the world.

Industry located in the Accra-Tema neighborhood attracts
workers from around the nation. It is a great melting pot of
different ethnic groups seeking jobs. Plastics manufacturing,
bauxite smelting, textiles, and oil refining are the major
businesses, drawing power supplies from the giant dam at
Akosombo.

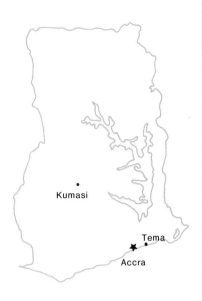

Kumasi, the seat of the Asante kings, is Ghana's
second largest city. The people wear both
traditional and Western clothes in everyday life.

KUMASI, THE SECOND LARGEST CITY

There are many other important cities in Ghana. Kumasi is the second largest, with over 350,000 residents. Located in central Ghana, it was the seat of the Asante kings beginning in the seventeenth century.

King Osei Tutu was Asantehene then, as the Asante rulers were called. He was looking for an ideal place to live. Osei Tutu ordered the great fetish priest, Okomfo Anokye, to find him a suitable home. According to legend, Okomfo Anokye planted seeds from the kum tree in two towns. Only one sprouted. In the Asante language, the word "si" means "survive." Therefore, "Kum-a-si" means "where the kum seed survived."

The other city, where the kum seed did not grow, is now the provincial town of Kumawu. In Akan, "wu" means "death." "Kum-a-wu" means "where the kum seed died."

The king didn't think it would be proper to build his capital where the kum seed had died, so he chose Kumasi for his palace. Kumasi is considered the garden city of West Africa. Flowers, boulevards, and landscaped yards are everywhere. Asante New Town, a suburb of Kumasi, is very beautiful.

Ghanaians can purchase almost anything they want at the recently constructed Asafo Market. It has everything from hardware supplies to produce. But some visitors to Kumasi think the older Central Market is more exciting. There are winding alleys jammed with shouting street vendors and crowded stalls. The noise level is high as buyers haggle with sellers. Each wants the best deal possible. Bargaining is a game that makes shopping fun. After a lot of arm waving and dickering, everyone is eventually satisfied with the final deal.

Right: The Asantehene   Left: A British fort in Kumasi

KUMASI, THE RELIGIOUS CENTER

Kumasi is also a religious center for the Asante people. Their year is broken into nine forty-two-day periods. Each period ends with a festival. The conclusion of the final period of the year is the Akwasidae Kese, the Great Akwasidae. On this day, the Asante king, the Asantehene, offers food and drink to the ancestors of his people.

These spirits are invited to Manhyia Palace where the Asantehene lives. Then there is a rigid ritual that the Asantehene must follow. If it is not performed exactly, the Asante think that bad luck will result. Epidemics, drought, forest fires, and bad harvests are only a few of the calamities that might happen. Therefore, the Asantehene is extremely careful.

On the day of the festival, the palace is crowded with guests. They represent captains from the old Asante army. This strong military force once controlled most of Ghana and almost defeated the British colonists. The Mamponhene is second in command to the Asantehene. He always has a place of honor. Other leaders include those of the twafo (the vanguard troops), the nifa (the right flank), the benkum (the left flank), the adonten (main body of soldiers), and the kyidom (the rear guard).

Even the gyasewahene, who were in charge of the treasury, are represented. Everyone wears his best costume, always made from elaborate kente cloth, a very expensive material, covered with woven designs handed down through the centuries.

After the official ceremonies, all Kumasi sings and dances. The streets are packed with people. Children are always brought along so they can see the Asantehene, and they are very well-behaved on occasions such as this.

Kumasi has many other attractions. The National Culture Center houses many items used by ancient Asante kings. Even gold weighing instruments and dust are exhibited.

Everyone tries to pull on the hilt of the Okomfo Anokye Sword. The sword was stuck into the banks of the Bantama River by a fetish priest in the court of Osei Tutu. According to legend, it marks the place where many Asante treasures are hidden. Supposedly, whoever pulls the sword from the stone will know the location of the treasure. No one has been successful yet. Of course, the sword isn't really a sword. It's a stone that looks like a blade. But it makes a great legend.

TWIN TOWNS

Some Ghanaian cities developed as "twin towns." For generations they might have been separate villages separated by a natural barrier, such as a river. In Akim Oda, for years the people on one side of a swamp were content to be independent of those on the other side. Finally, everyone figured that since they had always been friends, they should make their togetherness more formal.

Abetifi is also a twin town. On one side was the local native community, on the other side was "Christian" town. The latter included homes for the missionaries, most of the schools, a seminary, and houses occupied by converts.

OTHER TOWNS

In other Ghanaian towns, the migrant merchants formed their own enclave away from the main community. These colonies were called "zongos." Since many of the tradesmen did not belong to the local ethnic groups, they preferred to keep to themselves. Many of the merchants, such as the Hausa, were Muslims so the mosque was an important building in the zongo.

The more important Ghanaian towns originated as trading centers. They were usually located at a crossroads or at a river crossing. Others grew up around a mining site or in a rich agricultural region, to serve the people who worked there. Some lucky communities always had the best of everything. Obuasi is still a center of cocoa farming, as well as gold mining. Takoradi and Tema are the only ports on the Gulf of Guinea where ships can dock in the harbor.

Traditional houses in the northern city of Tamale

The regions of Ghana and their capitals

Some towns, however, were not very lucky. They might have been ports on a river, but were bypassed when highways and railroads were built.

POLITICAL DIVISIONS

Ghana is divided into districts. Their capitals are Koforidua (Eastern Region), Ho (Volta Region), Cape Coast (Central Region), Sekondi (Western Region), Bolgatanga (Upper East Region), Wa (Upper West Region), Tamale (Northern Region), Sunyani (Brong-Ahafo Region), Kumasi (Asante Region) and Accra (Greater Accra).

Overseeing all these regions is the People's National Defense Council, with its chairman as head of state. There currently is no legislature and the Supreme Court has been abolished. Members of the council are governmental ministers.

67

Ghana's flag (left) and coat of arms (right)

A National Investigation Committee checks into corruption. The government wants to be sure there is not a return to the old days, when many officials took bribes and stole money. The Citizen's Vetting Committee has been established to punish those who evade taxes, a very serious offense in Ghana.

GHANA'S FLAG AND COAT OF ARMS

Ghana's flag is red, gold, and green in equal horizontal stripes, with a five-pointed black star in the center of the gold stripe. Red represents the blood of Ghanaians who fought and died for independence. The gold symbolizes mineral wealth, and the green indicates the rich forest. The star represents freedom, signifying that Ghana was the first star, or nation, in Black Africa to achieve independence.

The nation has an interesting coat of arms. It is a shield divided into four quarters by a cross rimmed with gold. In the top left corner is a ceremonial sword with a linguist stick. The stick was carried by chiefs' translators as a badge of office. It represents local government. In the top right-hand corner is a castle, referring to

The chief (left) and a fetish priestess (right) during the Homowo celebration

national government. A cocoa tree and a mine shaft are in the bottom two quarters. They represent the country's natural riches. Ghana's motto, "Freedom and Justice," is also on the coat of arms.

HOLIDAYS

Like all nationalities, Ghanaians love holidays. It is a chance to get away from work and school, to relax and to meet friends. Ghana celebrates several national holidays: New Year's Day (January 1), Independence Day (March 6), Republic Day (July 1), Boxing Day (December 26), and Revolution Day (December 31). If a public holiday comes on a Saturday or Sunday, the following Monday is a free day. Nobody has to go to work or to school.

There are dozens of ethnic festivals, as well. Most are religious events. The Muslims in the north celebrate Damba in May and June. The Ga of Accra celebrate Homowo in August. The Bono people celebrate their apoo yam festival after the first yams of the year are harvested. There are many other festivals and local holidays.

Each is a serious way to observe Ghana's past. The love of history and tradition is important to all Ghanaians. It gives them a solid base from which to step into the future.

Chapter 6

HAVE A CUP 'A COCOA!

It's hard to think of anything tastier than a chocolate bar or a cup of hot cocoa. Maybe some Ghanaian children harvested the cocoa you eat. Ghana produces almost a third of the world's cocoa supply. It is the country's major cash crop. Today, Ghana is the Cocoa Coast. Thousands of tons of cocoa beans are shipped annually around the world.

Working on the cocoa plantations is a good way to earn extra money. Many Ghanaians start when they are only eleven or twelve years old, clearing brush from around the cocoa trees. Farmers also hire youngsters to care for the trees and to assist in the harvest.

The Asante region of Ghana is perfect for growing cocoa trees. It has the right climate and soil conditions. Everywhere are stands of trees—alongside fields and vegetable patches. Although Ghana produces some of the highest quality cocoa in the world, the crop is not native to Africa. It originated in South America. Over the centuries of European exploration, some settler brought cocoa pods to the tiny Spanish island of Fernando Po in the Gulf of Guinea.

Opposite page: Cutting cocoa pods

In 1878, Tete Quashie, a Ghanaian blacksmith working for the Spaniards, came home for a vacation. He had one cocoa pod tucked in his pocket. Tete Quashie planted the seeds from that pod in Akwapim, about thirty miles (forty-eight kilometers) north of Accra. Soon other farmers wanted to try out the new crop, and cultivation quickly spread.

Although cocoa remains important, it has one negative factor. Over the years, much of Ghana's natural forest cover has been destroyed to make room for cocoa trees. Sometimes the trees were planted in areas that could only support the fragile tropical ecosystem. Not only did the cocoa trees fail to grow, but the original jungle also was ruined forever.

HARVESTING AND MARKETING COCOA

Cocoa pods are knocked from trees by huge knives, called cutlasses, attached to long poles.

Ripe cocoa pods are from 8 to 15 inches (203 to 381 millimeters) long, shaped like cucumbers. Their golden rinds are leathery and tough. A sharp whack from a cutlass is needed to open the pod. An expert cutter can slash up to five hundred pods an hour.

Inside the pod are twenty to fifty beans enclosed in a gummy liquid. Some large pods might hold one hundred beans. Each bean is encased in a shell. After the pods are chopped down, they are carried to a central location on a cocoa plantation. There, after the pods are opened, the beans are separated from the pod by hand. The beans are then wrapped in leaves, where they can ferment in their own enzymes for a few days. Then the leaves are removed and the beans are spread on a platform to dry. Workers often stir

A workman cutting cocoa pods from the tree

and sift the beans for even drying. After several weeks, the cocoa beans have turned a dark brown color.

The hardest part of the harvest is next. The beans are bagged and the heavy bags are carried from the plantation to the closest village, where the harvest is picked up by government trucks.

For their labor, clearing brush and carrying heavy bags of beans, workers do not earn much money. They evenly divide what they earn. They also can get food from their own or their families' gardens.

In the village, an official of the Ghanaian Cocoa Marketing Board offers a price for the beans, depending on their quality. The top-rated beans are fully dried and firm. They are weighed, bagged, and hauled by truck to the closest railroad station.

Eventually, they find their way to a port and are shipped to the United States, Holland, United Kingdom, West Germany, and the

Left: Farmers working in their field   Right: Cassava, a root vegetable

Soviet Union. These are the biggest customers for Ghanaian cocoa.

About 200,000 tons of high-grade cocoa is produced each year in Ghana. Ghanaian agronomists and scientists are always working on ways to improve the crop and protect it from disease. Some Ghanaians have studied farming techniques in other countries. They then return home to put their education to good use.

FARMING

Almost 70 percent of Ghana's people are farmers, timber cutters, or employed in similar agricultural occupations. The average size of a farm is only five acres (two hectares). Crops that grow well in Ghana are cassava, sugarcane, maize, millet, yams, sorghum, tomatoes, tobacco, coffee, sweet potatoes, rice, rubber, cotton, cashew nuts, pepper, and ginger.

Many Ghanaians have animals on their farms. Almost two million goats and eleven million chickens are raised in the

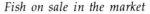
Fish on sale in the market

country. Ghanaian farms also breed one million cows, like the rugged Brahman cattle that can withstand the tropical weather.

Rabbit raising was begun in 1970. Because rabbits are fast growing animals, it is hoped that their meat will provide a quick and valuable source of protein for Ghanaians. The National Rabbit Project is located at Kwabenya, near Accra. Rabbits breed rapidly, so the program is well on its way toward being a success.

FISHING

The Gulf of Guinea is rich in fish. Canoes brave the stormy surf to haul in sardines, tuna, bream, and mackerel. Nets are tossed overboard and hauled in by hand. Lake Volta is good for fishing as well. More than 24,000 fishermen live along the shoreline in over nine hundred fishing villages. The tiny communities were built by the government since the dam at Akosombo was completed.

It is easy to bring fish to the dinner table even in northern

Ghana, far from the sea. Fish farms have been established there. It is now only hours from the time fish is "harvested" before a fresh catch lands in a shopping bag.

Men, women, and children work on the farms and plantations in Ghana. Women, however, are usually the ones who bring the goods to market. They use trucks called "tro-tros" that putt-putt their way from the farm loaded with goods to sell. It is hard to win an argument over prices with a Ghanaian farm wife. She is a sharp bargainer.

INDUSTRIES

Although Ghana is primarily an agricultural nation, there is industry as well. The government eagerly seeks investors by offering many incentives. There are four basic ways businesses are operated in Ghana.

First are the state enterprises, owned by the government. Next are private industries, owned either by Ghanaians or foreigners. Joint state/private ownership is also popular. This system is used when the government needs the help and advice of foreign technicians. Cooperative businesses are owned collectively by several Ghanaians pooling their money.

Foreign companies with plants and investments in Ghana include Kaiser Aluminum, Reynolds Aluminum, Union Carbide, Star-Kist, Agri-Petco, Texaco, and Mobil.

Gold has been mined in Ghana since people first started using gold for money and decoration. The richest mine is at Obuasi. One shaft plunges 1,000 feet (305 meters) into the ground. The tunnels are well lighted so the workers can see. Other mining sites are located at Tarkwa, Prestea, Dunkwa, and Konongo. Ghana has

Left: Gold ornaments from the early nineteenth century
Right: Bauxite is used in this aluminum smelter.

126,000,000 pounds (57,000,000 kilograms) of gold waiting to be dug from the ground. The government is considering opening fourteen new mines to tap this treasure.

A huge diamond mine is located at Oda in the Eastern Region and in the Bonsa area of the Western Region. Products from the mines can be seen in Ghana, a real jewelry showcase.

Manganese, a grayish-white metal used in the manufacturer of iron and copper alloys, is also a valuable resource. So is bauxite, an ore from which aluminum is made. One offshore oil field has been discovered.

Ghana's industrial base is very diversified, compared with that of some other African countries. Plants produce textiles, tires, and consumer goods. Buses, trucks, and cars are also assembled in Ghana.

INTERNATIONAL COOPERATION

For a time after independence, the government had trouble with mismanagement of money reserves. It became difficult to repay loans from other countries, especially in the worldwide business slowdown in the 1970s. To complicate matters, Nigeria ordered more than a million Ghanaians working in that country to go home. They subsequently had to be absorbed into the tight Ghanaian labor pool. Many found if difficult to get scarce jobs.

Working with the International Monetary Fund, the Ghanaian government is trying economic reforms. When this is accomplished, the country hopes to get development loans from the World Bank and from foreign commercial banks.

Ghana is active in the United Nations and its specialized agencies. Ghanaian soldiers served in the United Nations peacekeeping force in the Congo and in Lebanon.

The Ghanaian commander, Major-General Emmanuel Alexander Erskine, was noted for his skill in getting along with religious factions in the civil war in Lebanon. He was very fair. He also was concerned for his soldiers and even arranged to have Ghanaian musicians perform for major holidays. It helped the men's morale, making them feel less lonesome away from home.

Since Ghana was the first African nation to gain independence after generations as a European colony, it is admired by many developing countries. It is active in the Organization of African Unity and the Economic Community of West African States. The government says it is nonaligned in international politics. It promises to have friendly relations with all nations regardless of ideology.

The United States and Ghana have long been friends. However,

A panel displayed at the Asante exhibit in the Museum of Natural History in New York.

relations were strained when the Provisional National Defense Council took power in 1981. The council said the revolution was going to end what they considered to be Ghana's economic dependence on industrialized Western nations. The leaders of the council thought that this dependence was the same as being a colony again. At first, the United States government was considered unfriendly toward Ghana because of its new political structure.

Lately, this situation has eased. Trade has increased. Most political differences have been put aside. After all, there are many links between Ghana and the United States. There have always been educational, economic, cultural, diplomatic, and scientific ties between both nations.

Thousands of Ghanaians live in North America. One famous personality claims to be the Queen Mother of the Asantes. She is Nana Yaa Boakyiwa. In New York where she lives, her American name is Miss Florence Mensah.

In October 1984, the Asantehene and some of his chiefs visited New York City and Washington, D.C. They opened an exhibition at the Museum of Natural History in New York, entitled "The Asante, The Kingdom of Gold." The magnificent display showed the history and achievements of the Asante kingdom.

The Peace Corps program celebrated its twenty-fourth anniversary in Ghana in 1985. Many of the workers from the United States are teachers. Others assist with rural development, agriculture, and fisheries.

Currently, 47 percent of Ghana's people are under fifteen. Unfortunately, one third don't reach the age of ten, because of health-related problems. Agencies such as UNICEF (United Nations International Children's Emergency Fund) are attempting to help. Village clinics are slowly making headway against disease. They offer educational programs on cleanliness, child care, and home economics as well.

EDUCATION

Children are supposed to go to school for at least ten years, starting from the age of six. They help on farms during weekends and on vacations. However, it is estimated that only about 30 percent of adults can read or write. This situation is changing, as more and more parents realize the importance of keeping their youngsters in school. Dropping out of school is not encouraged.

After all, education is free and compulsory until age sixteen. Students attend a six-year primary course, followed by five years of junior secondary classes. Next comes two years of upper-secondary school called "sixth form," or students can take a two-year teacher training course or a technical course. There is a competitive examination at each level.

Young Ghanaians want to do well in their classes. If their grades are good, the young Ghanaians can apply for admission to one of the three universities in Ghana. They are the University of Ghana at Legon, the University of Science and Technology at

The University of Ghana is part of one of the best educational systems in the Gold Coast area of Africa.

Kumasi, and the University of Cape Coast in the Central Region.

The universities were closed during student riots at the outset of the most recent revolution. However, they have reopened and are preparing Ghanaians for many professional responsibilities.

Students are always eager to learn environmental studies and conservation. They want to deal with drought, grassland fires, deforestation, and other agricultural difficulties affecting Ghana.

The government is supporting a research-oriented system of education. Students are encouraged to use their knowledge in the countryside to help the people—and the future of Ghana.

The observance of ceremonies is important even in modern-day Ghana.

Chapter 7

RITUALS AND LIFE-STYLES

One observer years ago wrote that Ghanaians "were addicted to ceremonies." He mentioned the festivals that marked planting and harvesting, birth, puberty, marriage, and death. In fact, all the important events of one's life were marked by singing and dancing. Even in the rush of today's world, ritual provides a tie with the past. The ritual connects the modern Ghanaian with his or her ancestors.

Ghanaian young people are keenly aware what these rituals mean. They know they are part of something larger than themselves. They know exactly where and how they fit into the society.

The Adae ceremony is one of the most important traditional Asante ceremonies. It is very important to honor ancestors, because they watch closely over the family and community. Adae is celebrated twice every forty-two days. The first ceremony, the Akwasidae, is held on a Sunday. The second, the Awukudae, is held twenty days afterward, always on a Wednesday. Anyone born on the Saturday before Akwasidae is considered very lucky.

On the preceding day, drums are beaten as reminders to the village that something special will happen soon. The chief's house

Left: A craftsman carves a stool for a ceremony.   Right: Most ceremonies open with music.

is carefully cleaned. Chairs or stools are placed out for the arrival of the spirits.

On the big day, the chief, who is called "nana," arrives early. He wears his old clothes, as a mark of humility and respect for the spirits. Palm wine is made available for the chief's visitors on the holiday. Even the spirits are offered a drink. The chief pours drops of rum or schnapps on the "spirit stools." The pouring of the liquor is accompanied by the chief's washing of his hands.

A sheep is slaughtered for a feast and its blood smeared on the stools. After eating, the proud chief must sit and receive guests all day. The ceremonies remind everyone of their common bonds in the village. A nana who ignores the ceremonies might be removed from authority.

As many people moved from the interior to the cities, some of these rituals were not followed. Yet, even urban Ghanaians are returning to their roots. The old rituals give them a sense of being somebody in the bustle of the modern 1980s.

Left: Fetishes are believed to have magical powers.   Right: Fetish priests

Ghanaian festivals, or "durbars," are links to the past. (Durbar is a Hindu word used by the British to mean a reception.) They are tied to a natural event, such as hunting season. There is much drumming and pageantry.

You could say that Ghana's independence day on March 6 is the most exciting durbar. There are always parades and speeches in the regional and district capitals. Independence Square in Accra is jammed. The residents assemble early so they can get a good view.

RELIGION

Ghanaians are very religious. They accept many different faiths. Many of the people still believe in their traditional gods and spirits. These are represented by objects, called fetishes, that are believed to have magical power. A fetish priest is responsible for taking care of these items. It is a highly respected task. The priest

All religions are tolerated. Ghanaians can follow the teachings of Christianity, Islam, or their traditional religions. The man at right is a Muslim.

is one of the most important members of the Ghanaian community. His advice is always valued by the chiefs and the people.

Among the Ghanaians there is a mixture of Christians and Muslims. On the whole, different religious groups exist peacefully side by side. For instance, a fetish priest might support the constuction of a new Christian school in his village. In a curious blending of traditional and modern ways, many festivals officially end on Sunday with Christian church services.

Even within one family, several religions may be practiced. Therefore, Christians and Muslims often attend celebrations with relatives who follow some other belief.

TRADITIONAL RELIGION

Traditional Ghanaian religions do not have a holy book such as a Christian Bible or Muslim Koran. There is a Supreme Deity who is surrounded by lesser spirits. The lesser spirits look after the people on earth.

Elders are highly respected. When they die their spirits are also worshipped. Shrines dot the countryside, where offerings are made. Some of the more important shrines are those of the gods Dente and Tano. There is often a shrine to one's ancestors in the village. It is not uncommon for family members to ask the blessing of the spirits before undertaking a new job, a trip, or naming a baby.

Ghanaians are very hospitable and concerned about others. Life is considered valuable, to be shared. Anything that has life is therefore held in respect. That includes plants and animals, as well as people. Even rivers and forests are revered because they hold life. Everyone is considered lucky to be born. As such, people are expected to take care of themselves, because "good life" has to be passed on to the next generation.

This attitude permeates all aspects of living. A farmer does the best job he can with his fields. He knows it is his duty to support his family. But he also wants to treat the land well because it holds life.

Sometimes, of course, mistakes are made, such as chopping down too many trees. Yet by learning better farming techniques, a farmer shows respect for the spirit of the earth.

MUSLIMS

Traders from Mali were mainly responsible for the spread of the Muslim religion, or Islam, to Ghana during the fourteenth century. A few Muslim warriors from other African kingdoms moved in to spread the religion of Islam, but most conversion was without force.

Muslims believe that God is Allah. The religion was begun by the Prophet Muhammad. Many of the people living in northern Ghana and in Accra are Muslims. A good portion of the recently arrived immigrants are Muslims, too.

Muslims follow strict prayer and dietary rules. They must try to visit the holy Muslim city of Mecca at least once in their lifetime. Mecca is in Saudi Arabia, thousands of miles northeast of Ghana. For centuries, Ghanaians made the hard trip by foot or camel across the Sahara Desert, into North Africa, and across Egypt to get to Mecca. Today, it is easier. They use airplanes.

CHRISTIANS

The Catholic Portuguese arrived only a short time after the Muslims. Priests accompanied the soldiers and merchants on their colonizing ventures. As other European powers arrived, more Christian missionaries tagged along. They represented many different faiths.

By the mid-1970s, some Ghanaians had traveled to Europe to study, and several were even ordained as Protestant clergymen.

One well-known minister was Jacobus Capitein, the first African to be ordained, in 1742. He translated prayers and hymns into Fanti, his native language.

One missionary said that Ghanaians make a prayer out of work. He was right. It comes naturally to a people who revere life.

MARRIAGES

Family structure is very important to the Ghanaian because it means continuance of life. Therefore, the marriage ceremony is

A wedding celebration in Tamale

one of the principal rituals in Ghana. Many years ago, a girl might be betrothed to a man through family arrangements. Today, young Ghanaians can usually marry whom they please.

However, there are modern families who haven't given up all traditions. For those who believe in the old ways, the young couple has to complete three things before getting permission for a wedding. First, the young man offers drinks to his girlfriend's mother and father. Then he asks if he is acceptable as a son-in-law. This is called "knocking on the door." If the parents of the girl approve, the man can "enter" and begin the second stage.

Here, he gives "thank-you presents" to the girl's family. The higher the status of the girl, the more expensive are the offerings. The gifts are distributed among the girl's relatives, who witness the engagement. This is called the "presentation." It shows that the young man appreciates the family's good work in bringing up

Women are important in everyday life in Ghana. They do various tasks (clockwise from above) such as cooking, minding children, washing, and sewing garments.

the girl. It indicates that he is glad she is of high moral character and therefore worthy of marriage.

In the third and last step, the man has to provide more presents, usually money. This time the girl is the recipient, and can use the money to buy clothes and cooking utensils. This ensures that the couple will have a good start in their marriage. After that, the couple are considered formally married.

Christian weddings are similar to those in Western nations. But many couples still go through the traditional three steps before going to a church for a blessing.

FAMILY LIFE

Extended families are the rule in Ghana. Relatives give advice in many matters. A husband depends on his father, mother, and sisters, as well as his wife. If they have moved away, married people try to keep in close contact with their home village. They can always be certain of a warm welcome when coming ''back home.''

The rural Ghanaian family is made up of parents, children, grandparents, uncles, aunts, and cousins. The family usually lives in a compound, with a shared space for cooking and eating.

Elders are considered wise because of their life experiences. Besides, little children respect the older people because they tell the best stories.

Most Ghanaian women work, as well as raising their families. The majority help on farms and work as traders. Even if they work at home as housewives, they raise vegetables or make craft items to sell. They are very busy.

Women usually handle the money in a Ghanaian family. But

Left: A child helps pound grain   Right: Students with their teacher

modern society puts a strain on women. Since more children are attending school, there often is not as much help around the house or farm. That means the mother often has to do more work. Traditionally, raising children was a group effort. Everybody in the extended family helped. Children were quickly absorbed into the community. But as families move to cities, this has changed somewhat and some of that togetherness has been lost.

Yet they are able to cope. Rural mothers often send their daughters to work for wealthy patrons in the cities. There they take care of children and assist with household chores. The girls are well paid, clothed, and fed.

Working women now prefer to have fewer children. More nursery schools and day-care centers are being constructed to assist mothers who have jobs outside the home.

Women of Ghana are in many professions, such as nursing (left), and many still wear traditional dress (right).

THE WOMEN OF GHANA

The government's Department of Social Welfare and Community Development operates fifteen Women's Training Institutes throughout Ghana. The facilities are equipped by UNICEF. This United Nations agency provides items for cooking and sewing classes. UNICEF also gives out instructional materials for child-care courses. Women can even learn soap making and pottery.

Women have long been active in Ghanaian social, economic, and political life. They campaign hard. They vote. They are in positions of authority.

In the mid-1980s, Joyce Aryee was made secretary for information in the Provisional National Defense Council. She was the official spokesperson for the government. Mrs. Susanna

Left: Making fufu *and palm nut soup   Right: Mending fishnets*

Alhassan and Mrs. Aanaa Enin were two of the seven members of the central council that governs Ghana. Mrs. Alhassan had been minister of social welfare before she gained her new job in the central council in July 1984.

As more and more women reach professional-level jobs, the role of women in Ghanaian society will be strengthened.

EVERYDAY LIFE

The workday begins early, usually by 7:30 A.M. Ghanaians want to get a lot done before the midday heat. The city workers take a two-hour lunch break, returning to their jobs when it becomes cooler.

Fishermen are always back to shore by noon. They have time to sort their fish before it gets too hot. Afternoons are spent in the shade mending nets and repairing equipment.

Left: A group of people gather for a funeral.   Right: An elaborately carved casket

Families gather at suppertime to talk about the events of the day. Everyone, even the youngest child, gets an opportunity to tell of his or her adventures. Bubbling bean stew makes a delicious supper. Beans, fish, and vegetables go into the pot. Afterward, the children help clean the dishes. Then they scurry off to do their homework or play while the adults chat. It's always early to bed, especially in the villages that don't have electricity. Lamps using kerosene or palm oil are used for light.

Funerals bring together family members from all over Ghana. It is a chance for younger cousins to meet, and for older relatives to renew friendships. Any bills for funerals are shared by the entire extended family. But funerals are not really sad affairs. There is drumming, singing, and dancing to celebrate the end of one life and the beginning of a life after death. The Ghanaians believe that the spirits of the deceased will look after them.

Today's Ghana is a subtle mixture of the old and the new. There is the traditional versus the modern, African ways versus Colonial influence. The country has been able to mix these ingredients and arrive at an exciting way of looking at life.

Most youngsters in Ghana, the same as youngsters everywhere, like to have their pictures taken.

Chapter 8

OF GAMES AND

FOLKTALES

GAMES

The youngsters stand in a circle in the schoolyard. They don't mind the warm afternoon. It is time to play kye kye kule, a sing-song game made up of nonsense words.

One of the boys dashes to the center of the circle. He is excited because he is the leader of the game. He places his hands on his hand and sings, "Kye, kye, kule" (pronounced che, che, koo-lay): The other players take the same position and repeat the words. Then the leader, with his hands on his shoulders, sings another verse. Everyone follows. More verses and silly postures come next.

At the end of the song, the leader falls down, as do the others. Quickly, without warning, the leader jumps up and tries to tag one of the other players. They laughingly try to get away. However, they can't run until the leader does. He snares another boy, who then becomes the leader, and the game starts over again.

Ghanaian youngsters have many such games that involve song and rhymes. Even if the words are made up, they are fun.

There are a lot of running games, such as da ga, or "the big snake." In this game, thirty or more children pretend they are a boa constrictor. They try to capture other children, thereby adding to the length of the snake's tail. This is a very fast game because nobody wants to be eaten by the boa.

Another favorite game is the mosquito. It involves "making" a mosquito out of string. First, you place a loop of string over both thumbs. Then turn your left palm away from you. With your right hand, take the two strings that run between the thumbs and wrap them around the back of your left hand, keeping the loops on both your thumbs. With your little finger, pick up the two strings running between your left thumb and index finger. Then pull tightly. With your left little finger, pick up the two strings that run around your right thumb and pull tightly again.

Be careful to keep all the strings on your fingers for this next step. Reach over the left hand with your right hand. Take the two strings you find there, carefully pull them over your four fingers, and extend your hands. The knot in the middle of the string is called the mosquito. To swat it, clap your hands and as you open them, bend your little fingers so the string slips over them. The mosquito is gone.

TRADITIONAL CULTURE

Music and song, folklore and drama have always been central to the lives of Ghanaians. However, when Ghana was a colony, much of the beautiful heritage of West Africa was ignored. The European governments who colonized Ghana thought their Western culture was better. Even some Ghanaians forgot their heritage and wanted to be like the Europeans.

Left: Ivory tusks are used as horns. They are played to announce that the Asantahene is coming out of his palace. Right: Drums are traditional instruments.

Not all the colonizers felt that was a good idea, of course. Two men helped keep local culture alive. In 1913, English writer R.S. Rattray published *Hausa Folklore and Customs*. That work was followed by *Asante Proverbs* in 1916 and *Akan-Asante Folktales* in 1930. He was worried that the proverbs and folktales would be lost if someone did not write them. Professor Charles E. Graves took folk songs and presented them in classical piano presentations during the 1930s.

Gaddiel Acquaah, an African composer of religious songs, wrote many Christian hymns rooted in traditional musical styles.

After Ghana became independent, the people wanted to recapture what they had lost. They knew this was necessary, if Ghana was to become a vibrant nation with a sense of history.

Even the Ghana Symphony Orchestra has done its part. Under the direction of the late Philip Gbeho, the orchestra performed many folk concerts. Gbeho wanted to show his people that they had a treasure trove of their own musical styles.

A carved mask (left) and a ceremonial ax (right) from the Ghana National Museum in Accra

Another Ghanaian musician, professor J.H. Nketia, a world renowned scholar, was named to the International Musical Council in 1962 for his work in preserving West African music.

Dr. Kobina Bucknor demonstrates how one Ghanaian used his talents in the traditional arts. He has a degree in veterinary parasitology from Cornell University in New York state. When he was a student, he studied African art. Eventually, he started painting. He is now one of Ghana's busiest artists. One of his designs was used on a UNICEF greeting card.

To help keep folk traditions alive, the government set up the Arts Council of Ghana. This operates under the Ministry of Education, Youth, and Culture. Its board is made up of artists, writers, and other specialists. The council promotes cultural activities, establishes craft programs, and advises schools on how to make Ghanaian children aware of their rich ethnic heritage. The council also organizes cultural exchanges with other countries.

Left: Water jugs at a public well in Bolgatanga   Right: An Asante weaving kente cloth

Festivals around the country showcase dance, poetry, crafts, and art. Each regional capital has a cultural center. Three new facilities have recently been built: the Arts Center, Accra; the National Cultural Center, Kumasi; and the Cultural Center, Tamale. Others are being built in Koforidua and Sunyani. They contain galleries, museums, and theaters. In keeping with the Ghanaian respect for their ancestors, each center has a shrine.

The Ghana National Museum in Accra also has an art gallery. A large lecture hall there offers programs, for young people, about Ghana.

The Ghana Monuments Board, another valuable supporter of Ghanaian tradition, is responsible for the care and upkeep of historical sites. These include castles, forts, and other buildings that might attract tourists, as well as tell Ghanaians about their history.

A filmmaker

COMMUNICATION

Ghanaians are slowly edging out of an oral storytelling tradition to that of the written word. Children are now reading more. The Central Library in Accra annually loans thousands of books. It also operates a countryside bookmobile service that trundles its bumpy way into the most remote regions of the nation.

Ghanaians like newspapers. The British colonizers left a strong journalistic tradition. The most important English dailies are the *Ghanaian Times* and the *Daily Graphic* in Accra and *The Pioneer* in Kumasi. Many magazines have short lives and are soon replaced by others. Some newspapers and periodicals are printed in local languages.

Radio Ghana, the official broadcasting station, presents plays, news, music, and reviews. It brings information even to the smallest villages. A radio in Ghana is a prized item. It brings the people of Ghana closer together.

The control-room engineer at the Volta Dam talks to a worker at a substation.

Television Ghana presents numerous programs, including those from overseas. One of the most popular shows is "Concert Party." It features Ghanaian bands, singers, and dancers.

LITERATURE

There is a keen sense of the dramatic among Ghanaians. Some plays are written in English and others in the major Ghanaian languages. The Arts Council often sponsors national tours of theatrical troupes and helps local amateur companies. Young people are encouraged to form theater clubs. In fact, there is a very good children's theater group in Accra, which is supported by the Arts Council. Many contemporary Ghanaian playwrights and novelists are becoming popular. A well-known female dramatist is Efua Sutherland who established the Kusum Players. The players travel all over Ghana.

Ghanaian writers are encouraged to join the National

The children of Ghana learn about their heritage from older people and teachers who tell them folktales and proverbs.

Association of Writers and Poets. The society meets with publishers, illustrators, printers, and booksellers to discuss story ideas. They also try to resolve problems in the industry.

Folktales and proverbs are rich Ghanaian treasures. Westerners have always been fascinated by these stories. One famous book containing 3,600 proverbs was published in Basel, Switzerland, in 1879.

Ghanaians enjoy words. Their speech is very picturesque. Sometimes, poems are accompanied by drumbeats. Children learn from listening to older people. The best storytellers are respected members of the community. They are the ones who have kept Ghanaian tribal life alive over the centuries. Many of the stories remind children of moral lessons, such as "It is the gluttonous bee that becomes stuck in the palm wine jug," or "You don't ask for a chair when you go to a village where the chief sits on the bare floor." Ghanaian children would be quick to understand the lessons.

Many stories deal with a person or animal who overcomes obstacles. The hero or heroine is more clever than bigger or stronger creatures. These tales demonstrate that it is more important to be wise than tough. Sometimes, in a story, a trickster gets caught in his own trap because of greediness or jealousy.

Ananse, the spider, is a favorite character. He always seems to be in trouble. Yet he always saves himself at the last minute by using his head.

SPORTS

The national sport of Ghana is soccer. Ghanaian teams are very powerful on the playing field. They usually do well in

Azumah Nelson, featherweight boxing champion

international tournaments. Youngsters are great fans of the Black Stars, the team made up of the best players in Ghana. Everyone hopes that the team qualifies for the World Cup, the top soccer tournament in the world, held every four years.

Excellent track and field athletes are trained in Ghana. They do well in sprints, relays, long- and triple-jump events. Some of the best Ghanaian track stars are sprinters, such as George Enchill, Fred Owusu, Phillip Attipoe, James Idun, Grace Bakari, Joe Appiagyei, J.W. Idun, Collins Mensah, and Charles Moses. William Amakye, Ansah Bekoe, and Francis Dodoo always do well in jumping events. Effie Daetz, Helena Opoku, and Bakari Djan are rising young track stars.

Boxing is also popular in Ghana. A strong team participated in the 1984 Olympics in Los Angeles, California. Taju Ake, Christian Kpakpo, Michael Ebo Danquah, Sulemana Sadik, Douglass Odame, and Amon Neequaye fought in the light, feather, bantam, welter, and light-heavy weight divisions. They called themselves the Black Bombers.

The promise of Ghana is in its young people.

In the mid-1980s, Azumah Nelson was the reigning African and British Commonwealth featherweight boxing champion. Young fans flocked to the Accra Sports Hall to watch Nelson work out. The youngsters dreamed of being coached by F.A. Moses, who propelled Nelson into the championship ring.

In 1982, Nelson defended his title against Salvador Sanchez of Mexico in a fight in Las Vegas, Nevada. His Ghanaian fans cheered themselves hoarse when they heard he had won.

The Ghana Amateur Athletic Association picks athletes to participate in the matches and games that sports-hungry Ghanaians love to follow. Thirty-four athletes trained in Kumasi before competing in the first All-Africa Athletic Championships in Casablanca, Morocco, in 1984. The twenty-one men and thirteen women did very well.

You might even say that Ghana as a nation is something like its athletes—running, jumping, and always moving ahead.

MAP KEY

Abodom	D2	Elmina	D2	Nkawkaw	C2
Aboso	D2	Enchi	D1	Nsaha	D2
Accra	D2	Esiama	D1	Nsawam	D2
Achiasi	D2	Fian	A1	Nsuta	D2
Ada	D3	Foso	D2	Nyakrom	D2
Afadjoto (mountain)	C3	Funsi	A2	Obuasi	C2
Aflao	C3	Ga	B1	Oda	D2
Afram (river)	C2	Gambaga	A2	Oti (river)	A,B3
Agogo	C2	Garu	A2	Pong Tamale	B2
Akosombo Dam	C3	Gawso	C1	Pra (river)	D2
Akrofuom	C2	Gold Coast	D1,2,3	Prampram	D3
Akumadan	C2	Gulf of Guinea	D1,2,3	Prang	B,C2
Akuse	C3	Gushiago	B2	Prestea	D1
Akwawa (mountain)	C2	Half Assini	D1	Pru (river)	D2
Anloga	D3	Hamale	A1	Pwalagu	A2
Apam	D2	Han	A1	Salaga	B2
Asafo	C2	Ho	C3	Saltpond	D2
Asamankese	D2	Hohoe	C3	Samreboi	D1
Asankrangwa	D1	Huni Valley	D2	Savelugu	B2
Asante	C2	Jasikan	C3	Sawla	B1
Asikuma	D2	Jinjini	C1	Sekoni-Takoradi	D2
Atebubu	C2	Kade	C2	Sekpiegu	B2
Awaso	C1	Karni	A1	Sene (river)	C2
Axim	D1	Kedjebi	B3	Sogakofe	C3
Bamboi	B1	Keta	D3	Suhum	C2
Bawku	A2	Keta Lagoon	D3	Sunyani	C1
Bechem	C1	Kete Krachi	C2	Swedru	D2
Begoro	C2	Kibi	C2	Tafo	C2
Bekwai	C2	Kintampo	B2	Tale	B2
Berekum	C1	Koforidua	C2	Tamale	B2
Bia (river)	C1	Komenda	D2	Tano (river)	C,D1
Bibiani	C1	Konongo	C2	Tappo	A1
Bimbila	B3	Kpandae	B2	Tarkwa	D1,2
Black Volta (river)	B1	Kpandu	C3	Techiman	C2
Bogoso	D1	Kpong	C3	Techimentia	C1
Bole	B1	Kujani Game Reserve	C2	Tefle	D3
Bolgatanga	A2	Kulpawn (river)	A2	Tema	D2,3
Bompata	C2	Kumasi	C2	Tepa	C1
Bui Dam	B1,2	Kwahu Plateau	C2	Tumu	A2
Cape Coast	D2	Kwamisa (mountain)	C2	Volta (river)	C,D3
Cape Saint Paul	D3	Kwesimintim	D2	Wa	A1
Cape Three Points	D1,2	Lake Bosumtwi	C2	Walembele	A2
Chereponi	A3	Lake Volta	C2	Walewale	A2
Daboya	B2	Larabanga	B2	Wenchi	C1
Daka (river)	B2	Larteh Aheneasi	D2	White Volta	B2
Damongo	B2	Maluwe	B1	Wiasi	A2
Djebobo (mountain)	B3	Mampong	C2	Wiawso	C1
Doninga	A2	Maso	C1	Winneba	D2
Dormaa Ahenkro	C1	Mim	C1	Yala	A2
Du	A2	Mole Game Reserve	B1,2	Yapei Tamale Port	B2
Duayaw Nkwanta	C1	Morno	B2	Yeji	B2
Dunkwa	D2	Mpraeso	C2	Yendi	B2
Dzodze	C3	Nandom	A1	Zabzugu	B3
Efiduasi	C2	Nasia	A2	Zebila	A2
Ejura	C2	Navrongo	A2	Zuarungu	A2

109

MINI-FACTS AT A GLANCE

GENERAL INFORMATION

Official Name: Republic of Ghana

Capital: Accra

Official Language: English. Six major Ghanaian languages are spoken: Twi, Ewe, Ga, Fanti, Hausa, and Dagbani. But in all, thirty-four African languages are used.

Government: The Republic of Ghana has a military form of government, under the direction of the Provisional National Defense Council. Its seven-member ruling committee oversees the various ministries. There is no consitution, nor are there political parties. Citizens over the age of eighteen can vote for local defense-committee representatives. The head of state is also head of the national council. There are nine political regions in the country that correspond to states.

Flag: The flag has horizontal red, yellow, and green stripes with a black star in the center of the yellow stripe symbolizing African freedom. The red stripe symbolizes the blood of those who died for independence; yellow (gold) symbolizes the mineral wealth of Ghana; and green, the forest regions.

Coat of Arms: The Ghanaian coat of arms is a shield divided into four quarters by a green cross rimmed with gold. In the top left quarter is a stick carried by chiefs' linguists. It is crossed by a ceremonial sword. This section represents local government. In the top right-hand quarter is a castle representing national government. A cocoa tree is in the bottom left and a mine shaft is in the lower right. Both represent the natural and mineral wealth of the country. A lion is in the center of the cross, indicating that Ghana remains a member of the British Commonwealth. A black star on the top of the shield represents African freedom. Ghana's motto, under the shield, is "Freedom and Justice." The shield is held by two eagles.

Religion: About 45 percent of the population holds traditional beliefs, 43 percent are Christians; 12 percent are Muslims.

Money: The basic unit of exchange is the cedi. In February 1987, about 142 cedis equaled one U.S. dollar.

Weights and Measures: Ghana uses the metric system.

Population: Estimated 1986 population—13,892,000; distribution, 60 percent rural, 40 percent urban; density 150 persons per sq. mi. (58 per km²). Estimated 1991 population—16,262,000.

Opposite page: Participants in an Akan tribal festival

Cities:

```
Accra . . . . . . . . . . . . . . . . . . . . . . . . . . . . . . . . . . . . . . . . . . . . . 840,000
Kumasi . . . . . . . . . . . . . . . . . . . . . . . . . . . . . . . . . . . . . . . . . . . 353,000
Tema . . . . . . . . . . . . . . . . . . . . . . . . . . . . . . . . . . . . . . . . . . . . . 169,500
Sekondi-Takoradi . . . . . . . . . . . . . . . . . . . . . . . . . . . . . . . . . . 110,000
```

GEOGRAPHY

Highest Point: Mount Afadjato, 2,750 ft. (885 m)

Lowest Point: Sea level

Rivers: The major river system is the Volta, with three branches: the Black, Red, and White. The White Volta and the Black Volta are in the north and east, and the Ankobra, the Pra, and the Tano rivers are in the south and west.

Lakes: The largest natural lake is Lake Bosumtwi, in central Ghana. The building of a dam across the Volta River at Akosombo created one of the largest man-made lakes in the world. Volta Lake extends from southeastern Ghana north to the city of Yapei, a distance of 325 mi. (520 km). The lake covers 3,283 sq. mi. (8,502 km²).

Forests: Tropical forest cover central Ghana, making up one of the largest concentrations of trees in West Africa.

Climate: Ghana has a tropical climate. Accra, in the south, has an average temperature of 80° F. (27° C). Northern Ghana has higher temperatures. Temperatures can soar to over 100°F. (38° C). Most of Ghana receives 40 to 60 in. (100 to 150 cm) of rain a year, with the heaviest rain in the southwest. Axim, a town on the Gulf of Guinea, receives over 80 in. (200 cm) of rain each year. Northern and eastern Ghana have severe dry spells from November to March.

Greatest Distances: North to south—400 mi. (644 km)
East to west—280 mi. (451 km)

Coastline: 290 mi. (466 km)

Area: 92,000 sq. mi. (238,279 km²).

NATURE

Trees: Common trees include African mahogany, African whitewood, and dense evergreens in the southwest. The northern savanna is covered with dense, tall Guinea grass.

Fish: Catches include herring, mackerel, soles, skates, sharks, mullet, bonitoes, crabs, lobster, and prawns.

Animals: Common animals include hyenas, antelope, wild hogs, chimpanzees, snakes, crocodiles, otters, lizards, tortoises, and giant snails.

Birds: Common birds include parrots, hornbills, kingfishers, eagles, herons, cuckoos, doves, and pigeons.

EVERYDAY LIFE

Food: In the fields the workers often hunt small game that can be prepared for lunch. A favorite dish is black bean stew, which contains vegetables, fish, and meat. In the rural areas cooking and eating are done in communal fashion, often with groups of families sharing the food and chores.

Housing: The urban cities suffer from overcrowding in many districts due to the influx of rural people seeking work. Government projects dot the suburbs. In rural areas, an extended family can include parents, grandparents, uncles, aunts, and cousins living in a complex of one-story homes. The houses are usually clumped around an open compound where the cooking and eating are done. In central and southern Ghana many of the people live in rectangular houses that have mud walls and thatch or tin roofs. Many of the people in northern Ghana live in round houses with mud walls and cone-shaped, thatch roofs.

Holidays:
January 1, New Year's Day
March 6, Independence Day
Good Friday
Holy Saturday
Easter Monday
July 1, Republic Day
December 25, Christmas Day
December 26, Boxing Day
December 31, Revolution Day

Culture: Writers in Ghana are encouraged to join the National Association of Writers and Poets. Ghanaians also enjoy drama, with troupes such as the Accra children's theater attracting many viewers. The Kusum Players tour the country with theatrical presentations. The Ghana National Orchestra and many regional orchestras are highly respected. Folktales and proverbs told by storytellers are traditionally popular. Many deal with Ananse, a spider who always outwits his larger opponents. The stories usually end with a moral. The National Cultural

Center in Kumasi is devoted to the Asante heritage. The Arts Council of Ghana is located in Accra and sponsors a variety of cultural programs.

Cultural life in Ghana has many affinities with that of the neighboring countries around it, festivals and rites are largely centered on chieftancy and the family. Dance, music, pottery, wood carving, weaving, and gold and silver smithing are popular cultural activities.

Communication: In addition to numerous African-language newspapers, there are several major English publications such as the *Daily Graphic* in Accra and the *Pioneer* in Kumasi. Newspapers are state owned, and news is strictly controlled. Radio Ghana is the official broadcasting station. The government-owned Television Ghana offers a variety of programs.

Transportation: Ghana has long been a trading crossroads with the rest of West Africa. Numerous roads crisscross the nation, most of them branching out from the coastal cities. Only a small portion of the country is served by rail, and most trains carry freight. Kotoka International Airport in Accra offers flights to major African and European cities.

Sports: The most popular sport in Ghana is soccer, which is called football. Track and field athletes are strong in international competition, as are Ghanaian boxers.

Education: Education is free and compulsory in Ghana, with at least ten years of schooling required. Adult literacy is only about 30 percent—one of the highest in Africa, however. Children start school when they are six years old. The system provides six years of primary school, followed by five years of junior secondary school. Pupils continuing in school can then take a two-year secondary upper-level course, a teacher-training program, or a technical course. If they qualify, they can then enter a college or university.

There are three universities: The University of Ghana at Legon, the University of Science and Technology at Kumasi, and the University of Cape Coast. Many university students also study in Great Britain, the United States, and other foreign countries.

Social Welfare: There are ministries in Ghana responsible for works and housing, youth and sports, rural development and cooperatives, education, labor and social welfare, among others. Many programs, such as the women's training institutes, have been developed with the assistance of the United Nations.

Health: Health problems are compounded by communicable diseases, poor sanitation, and poor nutrition. Hospitals and clinics are provided by the government and by Christian missions.

Principle Products:
Agriculture: cocoa, coffee, rubber, rice, vegetables, livestock
Fishing: sardines, bream, mackerel, tuna
Manufacturing: textiles, vehicles assembly, crafts
Forestry: mahogany, sapele, utile

Names: It is simple to tell the day of the week on which a Ghanaian was born. The following table explains the "day" names of the Akan people, who comprise the bulk of Ghanaian ethnic groups in the central part of the country.

English	Akan	Male Name	Female Name	Meaning "child of"
Sunday	Kwasida	Kwesi	Akosua	the sun
Monday	Dwowda	Kwadwo	Adwoa	peace
Tuesday	Benada	Kwabena	Abena	fire
Wednesday	Wukuda	Kwaku	Akua	fame
Thursday	Yawda	Yaw	Yaa	strength
Friday	Fida	Kofi	Afua	growth
Saturday	Memeneda	Kwame	Amma	most ancient

Therefore, a boy or girl might have a Christian name and a day name as well as a family name. For instance, Kwadwo Joseph Mensah was born on a Monday. His Christian baptismal name is Joseph and his family name is Mensah. The same is true for Yaa Rachel Anna, born on a Thursday.

Virtually no Akans are Muslims, so a Muslim child has a traditional Islamic first name plus a family name. A non-Christian Akan child would have a day name and a family name.

IMPORTANT DATES OF WEST AFRICAN HISTORY RELEVANT TO GHANA

Stone Age (1200 B.C.) — Migrations into Ghana

A.D. 300s to 1000s — Settling of ancient black kingdoms of Ghana

1200-1700 — The empire of Mali becomes the largest of all kingdoms of West Africa

1300s — Mansa Musa rules the Mali kingdom for twenty-five years; settling of ancient kingdom of Bono

1400s — Songhai kingdom becomes dominant in West Africa

1471 — Portuguese land on Gold Coast

1482 — Portuguese build Castle of Sao Jorge da Mina at Elmina

1553 — English explorer Thomas Windham charts Ghana coastline

1591 — Battle of Tondibi; Songhai empire crushed by Moors

1598 — Dutch begin construction of forts along Gold Coast

1600s — Black kingdom of Asante spreads power; city of Kumasi built

1631 — English slave traders enter Gold Coast market

1807 — Britain's Parliament outlaws slavery, beginning the disintegration of the slave trade

1821 — British government takes control of private trading company operating Gold Coast settlements

1826-1900 — Asante wars against the British

1844 — Fanti chiefs approve the Bond of 1844, giving British incentive to defeat the Asante

1850 — Missionary societies come to Ghana; Danes leave Ghana

1870s — Basel Mission Society establishes ninety schools; other mission groups arrive in Gold Coast

1872 — Dutch pull out of Ghana; British make Gold Coast a crown colony; Asante war begins

1874 — British Asante war ends; Southern Ghana becomes a British crown colony

1877 — Seat of colonial government moves from Cape Coast to Accra

1896 — Asante confederation dissolved; Agyeman Prempeh I, the Asante king, is exiled; Aborigines' Rights Protection Society formed

1898 — Northern territories become British protectorate

1901 — Asante kingdom made a British colony

1918 — British Togoland formed out of former German colony

1919 — All Ghana made into British crown colony of the Gold Coast

1930 — Achimota School in Accra founded

1946 — British Togoland becomes United Nations trust territory

1947 — United Gold Coast Convention (UGCC) formed; UGCC asks Kwame Nkrumah to be its general secretary

1949 — Nkrumah forms the Convention People's party (CPP)

1950 — Nkrumah is jailed

1951 — Constitution calling for a legislature is written

1952 — Nkrumah becomes prime minister of the Gold Coast

1954 — Constitution is formally adopted and a cabinet composed of Africans is established

1956 — British Togoland becomes part of Gold Coast

1957 — Gold Coast becomes first black nation in twentieth century to win independence (on March 6); called Ghana

1958 — Preventive Detention Act passes, allowing detention without trial for five years

1960 — New republic constitution adopted

1964 — Nkrumah establishes one-party rule

1966 — Kwame Nkrumah is deposed in military coup

1969 — Return to civilian rule under new constitution

1971 — Devaluation of Ghanaian currency leads to unrest

1972 — Military coup led by Colonel I.K. Acheampong; Nkrumah dies

1975 — National Redemption Council replaces Supreme Military Council

1977 — Political parties outlawed; riots result

1978 — Military coup deposes Acheampong

1979 — Military coup deposes Lieutenant-General Frederick Akuffo; new constitution written, Dr. Hilla Limann elected president

1981 — Military coup deposes Limann; constitution suspended; Provisional National Defense Council, led by Jerry Rawlings, established

1987 — Permanent memorial to black American scholar and civil rights leader W.E.B. DuBois erected in Accra

IMPORTANT PEOPLE

Gaddiel Acquaah, composer of religious songs based on traditional music styles

Anthony William Ado, first Ghanaian to receive a Ph.D., from the University of Wittenberg in eighteenth century

J.E.K. Aggrey, educational leader in twentieth century

Kobina Bucknor, artist and pianist

Jacobus Elisa Johannes Capitein, first African ordained as Christian minister (1742); translated hymns and prayers into his native Fanti language

J.E. Casely-Hayford, African member of Legislative Council in early twentieth century

J.B. Danquah, a founder of and leading figure in the United Gold Coast Convention

Philip Gbeho, director of the Ghana Symphony Orchestra

Jakpa, ruler of Kingdom of Gonja, 1622-1623 to 1666-1667

Anne Ruth Jiagge, first woman lawyer in Ghana; Supreme Court justice; vice president of the executive committee of the World YMCA; chairperson of the United Nations Commission on the Status on Women

Azumah Nelson, African and British Commonwealth featherweight boxing champion in the 1980s

J.H. Nketia, international music scholar

Kwame Nkrumah (1909-1972), first prime minister and president of Ghana

Osei Tutu, founder of Kingdom of Asante (Ashanti) in 1680s

Prempeh I, Otumfuo Sir Agyeman, (1870?-1924) last independent Asantehene (king of Asante); sent into exile by British in 1896

Reverend Philip Quague, African, ordained in England, who founded first modern school in Cape Coast in 1766

Jerry John Rawlings, chairman of the Provisional National Defense Council and head of state; led revolution that took over in Ghana in 1981

Efua Sutherland, writer; dramatist; founder of Kusum Agoromba (Kusum Players) drama society

Opposite page: Asante chief in ceremonial robes

INDEX

Page numbers that appear in boldface type indicate illustrations

About the Author

Martin Hintz, a former newspaper reporter, has written more than a dozen books for young people. The subjects range from training elephants to other social studies titles included in the Childrens Press Enchantment of the World series. He and his family currently live in Milwaukee, Wisconsin. Hintz has a master's degree in journalism and is a professional travel writer/photographer who has won numerous awards for his work.

The author would like to thank the following individuals and organizations for their assistance in researching and reviewing Enchantment of the World, Ghana: Professoror Peter Osei-Kwame and William Denevan, University of Wisconsin-Madison; UNICEF; US Committee for UNICEF; K. K. Jehanfo, Ghana Mission to the United Nations; United Nations Environment Program; the Embassy of Ghana; Kwamina B. Dickson; J. M. Assimeng; and Walter Birmingham, I. Neustadt, and E. N. Omaboe, editors of *A Study of Contemporary Ghana*.